eighteen years

written by
Madisen Kuhn
with illustrations by Laura Supnik

Eighteen Years

Cover & illustrations by Laura Supnik.
pp. 1, 5, 9, 91, 135, 165, 189, 209, 221, 237, 249, 256, 266
For art inquiries, contact lsupnik@gmail.com.

Illustrations digitally traced by Christian Gale.
Connect with him on Instagram: @christianegale

ISBN 978-1-4351-6588-5

Dedicated to my followers—

Thank you for all the kindness and support you have shown me over the years. I will never be able to truly express how much it means to me. Your precious souls are a constant reminder that I am never alone.

I love you endlessly.

Dear Friend,

Growing up is scary. I've learned that it is never what you expect it to be. Who I imagined myself to be as a teenager was not who I was. I remember when I was ten years old, I wrote a letter to my future self. I folded up the note and put it in a yellow envelope and it sat in my underwear drawer for years. I asked all the important questions: are you popular? Do you have a boyfriend? Do you kiss him?

At sixteen, I encountered things I could've never imagined: dropping out of public school, battling depression, and I still hadn't had my first kiss. (Which, by the way, is totally normal and totally not a big deal. It didn't happen till I turned eighteen. It wasn't like the movies, but I liked it and who it was with. Don't rush anything. Don't regret anything. You have time.) Time has a tendency of never passing at a consistent speed. Sometimes, everything is so slow that you feel like you're frozen in place, and sometimes everything is so fast that you can't seem to catch your breath. But it's always there, and it will never stop moving forward.

These pages hold my scattered thoughts and feelings over the past few years. And in these years, I've learned so much. My late teens have been a time of incredible growth. I learned that what I thought were endings, really were not. And when true endings came, they were good, and right, and really new beginnings. I learned the importance of independence. The importance of never letting fear win. The imperativeness of leaping outside of my comfort zone and forcing myself to stay there. I learned that emotions lie. That emptiness is not permanent. That people come and go. That change is inevitable, unavoidable, and good.

Writing has forever changed me. It has aided me in letting go, forced me to be honest with myself, and opened my eyes to the fickleness of feelings. It has helped me communicate when my voice falls short, allowed me to sleep better at night, and it has taught me to not be afraid of sharing myself with others. I encourage you to try it. Even if you think you aren't "good," do it for you. Write, even if no one else ever reads it. Write because you owe it to yourself to experience the freedom of ranting in ink, crumbling up the paper, throwing it in the trashcan, and feeling like you can finally breathe again.

Growing up is an adventure. You will encounter things no one really warned you about, but you will wing it, and find a way to get through it, and you will come out stronger than before. You will find people who will help you out along the way. You will meet people that change you forever. You will cry because you feel stuck. You will dust yourself off and try again. You will drive with the windows down, hair blowing in the wind, and laugh because you didn't know life could ever feel this beautiful. People will hurt you, leave you, and complicate you. You will use this as an excuse to not love yourself. You will tell yourself you don't deserve love. You will learn that this is a lie.

Growing up is beautiful. I have never felt more alive than I do today. And it's because I've lived through all the mess and pain of the preceding years. Mess and pain causes us to grow, and growth is one of my favorite parts of life. We can be better if we choose to put in the effort. We have so much more control than we think. It has taken me awhile to realize that. I still struggle with feeling powerless. I'm still so far away from being who I want to be. But every morning, we have the ability to wake up and decide to be whole. We can decide to love ourselves, to love the people around us, and to never give up on being the best possible versions of ourselves.

So, here's to finding your way. Here's to falling in love. Here's to falling out of it. Here's to loving yourself. Here's to untangling anxiety and declaring it powerless. Here's to feeling at home. Here's to always wanting to be better. Here's to never giving up on becoming the person you know you are capable of being.

Here's to growing up.

All my love,

m.k.

winter
2012-2013

bitter bits better

you clutter my mind
thoughts of you, thoughts of me with you
thoughts that keep me from rest
that lull me to sleep at night
your words are like butter
they're smooth and they're rich
and they make the bitter bits better

p a l i n d r o m e

you hurt me.
you are the moon that controls
the tides of my eyes
you are a dark moon
with thousands of craters
thousands of imperfections
i have imperfections too,
but the difference is:
i think you hate me while
                    i love you.

favorites

ask me who my favorite artists are
ask me what my favorite season is
ask me where my favorite memories lie

ask me where i'd love to go,
what i'd love to see,
why i cut my hair the way i do,
who i desire to be

i want you to ask me these things
because perhaps
my answers will make you
fall in love with me

i surely fell in love with you
whilst you were listing off
your favorites

catharsis

i love good cries,
loud sobs that soak your pillow
the kind that come at the end
of a perfect book

you're gasping for air
as droplets of salt water
trickle down your cheeks
into the corners of your mouth
as your chest rises and falls
and your vision is blurred
by the tears

but your mind is so clear
and your every thought
in that moment
feels so meaningful
and important and right

it feels okay to just
let it all out
it makes you feel like
you are free

everything but

you fell in love with
late nights and soft kisses,
holding hands,
phone calls ending in
"i love you more."

you fell in love with
someone knowing you
as well as you know yourself,
being seen when you
thought you were invisible,
comfortableness

you fell in love with
sparking short fights and
make up "i love you"s,
silent car rides and
quiet understandings

but you did not
fall in love
with me

g e m

i find beauty not in your lips,
but in the soothing words that separate them
and your eyes aren't stunning
because they are blue, but because
they found me
when i had tried to stay hidden
and you don't have a clue
how special you really are

you are as sweet as sugar
you are real
you are different
a soft petal crowded by thorns
treasure amongst dust

and i find it so beautiful
that someone like you
could love me

n o t i c e   m e

i want to be noticed
by a stranger with tender eyes

i want to be seen, biting my lip
or pushing my glasses
up the bridge of my nose

i want to be thought of days later
wondered about who i am
and what i hold dear

i want to be noticed
as much as i notice

because i see them
and they see me

to them,
i am just another face

but to me,
they are a mysterious masterpiece

i. haiku

with you, 4am
is not lonely and i do
not mind long car rides

who are you, really?

who are you,
really?

you are not a name
or a height or a weight
or a gender,
you are not an age
and you are not
where you are from

you are your favorite books
and the songs stuck in your head,
you are your thoughts
and what you eat for breakfast
on saturday mornings

you are a thousand things,
but everyone chooses
to see the million things
you are not

you are not
where you are from
you are
where you're going
and i'd like
to go there
too

v i o l e t s   a r e   b l u e

i look at you
and i can see it in the contours
of your solemn face

you think you hide it,
but i see you

i see the hurt
the dark circles beneath your eyes
and the quiet plea
dancing on your bottom lip,
too afraid to be voiced
too afraid to be heard
because you're too afraid
of being hurt

and i just want to take you
and wrap you up in my arms
hold you, console you
tell you things that you'll believe,
but you don't seem to believe
anything, anymore
because you have been deceived
too many times

so i'll just look at you
and see the pain in your fake smile,
and i'll smile back

and i'll hear the attempted deception
when you tell me that you're just tired,
and i'll say me too

i know you're broken inside
i can see it
violets are blue,
and so are you

ii. haiku

you can either let
it eat you up inside, or
you can conquer it

r a i n

there are so many types of rain
light rain, heavy rain
spring rain, summer rain

the kind of rain
that makes you want to
curl up with a good book,
the kind that races down
your car window
as you look out at
the tall trees whizzing by

rain that you kiss in,
rain that makes you feel alone

sometimes it smells of
new beginnings,
and sometimes it feels like
you're drowning

and then eventually
it stops
and you can hardly remember
if you even like rain
at all

u n d e f i n a b l e

i can't describe the feelings i get
the day after a rainstorm
or when the sun sets early
in the winter

happiness and sadness
are easy to recognize,
but sometimes i have emotions
that i cannot identify

like how i feel
about you

secrets

some are hidden
by long sleeves
and baggy sweatshirts,
behind bloodshot eyes
and stale breath,
written in light graphite
on crinkled sheets
in shoeboxes,
therapy sessions,
and 2am text messages

iii. haiku

you are my thoughts as
the sun rises, and my dreams
after it has set

a w a k e n i n g

i long for a life i have control of

i want a space of my own, decorated
with photos that hold nice memories,
soft pillows, and scented candles

i want shelves filled with books of
adventure and poetry

i want to wake up every morning
excited for what is to come

i want to look up at the sky
and feel the sun warm my face

i want to go on long walks and hikes
and feel healthy and strong
i want to feel productive and satisfied
i want to take more photographs
and take up new hobbies

i want to become friends with
more interesting people
who will tell me stories about
places i've never been

i want to feel alive

c r y

i cry to feel emotion
to sympathize
to confirm my mortality
to express joy,
to release bottled up
hate
sadness
guilt
but the worst is when
i cannot cry

i beg the tears
to trickle down my face,
only for me to wipe them away

the absence of them
makes me feel like my sentiments
aren't true
they're fraud
       phony
          insincere

if i can't even control
or understand
my own tears,
how can i expect someone
to dry them for me
when i can't explain
why they're present in one moment
and absent in the next?

sticks and stones

i love your laugh
all your little quirks
cute nicknames you've given me
and our late night confessions

but i don't want to

because one moment
i feel euphoric
and the next
i don't even know who you are
you are not my sunrise
or brisk winter day

this constant turmoil
of affection and disdain
has frozen my heart

it is too much
for me to bear

sticks and stones
may break my bones,
but you will always hurt
the most

c r u s h

i'm too shy
to tell you how i feel

so i'll hide behind
timid smiles
and soft hellos

i'm afraid
if i ask you
"what do you think
of me?"
your reply will be

"i don't."

don't blink

it's a peculiar feeling
waking up after it's rained
the world never ceases to exist
so many things
happen
while your
eyes
are shut

maybe that's why i don't sleep
(i don't want to miss anything)

iv. haiku

i want to be who
you want me to be: someone
who isn't afraid

i love you all day long

you only tell me
how you feel late at night
when you're in bed
and your eyes
are blurred with sleep

i think it's because
you feel more hidden at night,
you wrap the darkness
around you like a blanket,
you find comfort
in the stars
and the quiet opacity

just be sure to love me
in the morning

jesus christ

there is someone
who loves me
despite my flaws,
despite all the terrible mistakes
i have made

he hears all the ugly thoughts
that inhabit my mind
he sees me in my darkest times
when i'm weak, doubtful
when i'm ready to turn my back

and this man,
he sees how imperfect i am
this perfect man sees all my wrongs
and this is what he tells me:

"to me, you are beautiful
to me, you are worth it
i know you're not perfect
i know you make mistakes,
but i will never turn my back on you
i will love you eternally
and i hope you can love me too."

a perfect man not only tells me
he loves me, he shows me
how much every single day

and this man,
he loves you too.

his name was house

when i'm sitting alone at night
in the quietness of my large and aging house
i hear so many noises i'm oblivious to
during the daylight

the clicks of the air conditioning
switching on and off,
the creaking of the floors and walls,
the subtle squeaking the fan makes
in the living room

it's as if my house is sighing
he's sighing at me
disappointed in me
he asks why i don't notice him during the day,
why i only notice him late at night
when i'm lonely and there are no
other noises to entertain my ears

i tell him that i'll try to listen more
closely in the morning, but then
i fall asleep and i wake up
and i do not remember
what i promised my sweet house,
so he continues to sigh all day long,
hoping that at some point, even if
it is late at night when i am lonely
and there are no other noises
to entertain my ears,
i will notice him again

if only for a little while

v. haiku

i don't feel well, but
the sound of rain on my roof
makes me feel better

vi. haiku

show me that you care,
i'm tired of guessing if
you love me or not

cover to cover

she buried her face in books
so no one could see
the emptiness in her eyes

she filled her mind
with fictional fantasies
and hoped that one day
they would become real

but because her head
was always stuck in a book
she never got the chance
to have adventures of her own

w h y , w h y , w h y

in the middle of the night
i think of you
and of how much
i miss you

but when i wake up
i get on with my day
and i don't think
of you at all
why?

distance makes the heart break

i want to be where you are
in your city
with the lights blurring past
as we ride in your car
going somewhere, anywhere
to your favorite restaurants
or to a concert of a band
we both love

it really doesn't matter
where we go
as long as i'm with you

i want to hold your hand
and smell the scent
of your cologne,
to see you smile back at me,
to hear your laugh,
to hear our laughs combine
and create a song all of its own

i want to be
where my heart is:
with you

loneliness

sometimes you feel it
when you're by yourself

separated, secluded
on your own

but it feels
the worst when
you are not

there are people
all around me,
but i feel
so
alone

t i r e d

my

body

wants

to

go

to

sleep

but

my

mind

does

not

this poem is not about you

you're asleep and i'm sad
i wanted to stay up all night
and talk with you
about your day
and why the sky is blue

everything is so easy with us
our words flow back and forth steadily
like the gliding of a ship
atop a calm sea

when i feel broken
you mend me with your words
when i have nothing to say
you effortlessly occupy the silence

you fill this gap inside me
in a way that makes me forget
i was ever incomplete

i'd tell you all of this,
but you're asleep

stop fading

how can i say this
so that you understand
exactly how much i miss you?

i feel an aching in my fingertips
that cannot be shaken
and i cling to the little bits
you've left behind

i try to picture what it was like
before you were gone,
but you're fading

i fear the day i wake up
and you are not
the first thing on my mind

i fear that one day
i will forget someone
who meant so much to me

imbalance

i want things to be simple

but they never are
with us

i'll always be wanting you
when i can't have you

you'll always have
someone better

cry for help

maybe i don't eat because
i want my skin
to be transparent
i want people to see me
for who i truly am
i hope to one day
wither away
until i am nothing
until i am just a pile of bones

maybe then you'll
notice me

unrequited

someone
fell in love with
my eyes
when they lit up
because of you

a grin like that
makes me weak
in the knees

too bad you're smiling
at her, not me

vii. haiku

it's 12:02 and
(could you be thinking of me?)
i'm thinking of you

may i be your wildflower?

it feels as if
i'm the one
always chasing
after someone

my lungs are burning
and my heart is tired,
i want to collapse
and loll here forever

let the flowers
bloom all around me
as i leave an imprint
in the grass

maybe someone
will gaze upon the blossoms
and mistake me for a lily

for jake

you are my koala,
my sunshine and my precious

your big green eyes hold
so much innocence,
they make me want
to curl you up
and hide you
someplace timeless

i love the way
you wrap your arms a
round my neck
and plant little kisses
on my cheeks

please stay this little
forever,
i never want you
to grow up

truth

i think the world
would be a nicer place
if we stopped pretending
we knew everything
about everyone

you noticed me

this feeling of ecstasy,
it blooms inside of me

sparks like fireworks
spread throughout my limbs
my hands quiver and
my heartbeat quickens

i want to run through
endless fields and shout
into the emptiness

because all of the sudden,
i am not invisible

shooting star

you are not mine,
but sometimes
i pretend that
you wish you were

i create this idea
that you secretly
want me

and i often forget
it's just something
i've made up

you do not want me,
and you are not mine

he loves me not

maybe if
i pluck the petals
from this flower
and the last one that
falls to the ground
says "he loves me,"
you will

anger

it will tear away
your skin,
gnaw on
your bones,
and set your soul
aflame

this hatred
inside of you
will spread
until you are
consumed
in a fiery rage
that should've been
extinguished
at its first spark

who will
come along
and save you?

who will
smother
your soul?

let me in

i've shown you
the depths of me
all the crevices
and trenches,
the incomplete
darks and lights
of who i am

but i don't think
you'll ever let me past
the surface
of who you are

c h e e r w i n e

i worry about you
(more than you know)
i see the decisions you make
(all the things you've done
that you'll soon see were mistakes)

do you know who you are?
(i don't think you do)
you're boundlessly wandering,
trying to find something (anything)
to mask your pain

i know
you know
that how you're living
will never quench
your thirst

i know
(deep down)
your soul is pleading,
"please, someone save me
from myself."

valentine's day

it is not about
ninety-nine cent cards,
from the dollar store,
or milk chocolate
in the shape of a heart

it is not about
feeling bad for yourself
because you're single
or going out
to an expensive dinner

it is not about
how many bouquets
or "happy valentine's day"
text messages you receive

love is beautiful,
it is forbearing and selfless,
it is not bitter or rude,
it is modest and humble

so even if you think today
was created by Hallmark
to sell cards,

why not show love
to someone
you care about?
or even to a complete stranger

you don't have to have
a boyfriend or girlfriend
or husband or wife
or a "significant other"
to celebrate today

because everyday
is a wonderful day
to love someone

m a s k s

please remember,

no one is as
strong
as they seem

no one is as
careless
as they pretend
to be

c o s m o s

i am a celestial body,
orbiting a star

my eyes are telescopes,
if you look into them
you can see
all my constellations
of thought

i harbor rivers and
oceans of aspiration,
i hold forests of curiosity,
deserts and islands
of loneliness,
cities of anticipation

not everyone takes the time
to look, to see me,
but
you do

i thought

what do you do
when you love someone
and you're bursting
literally bursting
to let them know

but you can't
because it's destructive

it's no good for you
and it's no good for me
i can't let go of it
i love you today
and tomorrow and i love
you past any thought
i could think up

it's wrong though,
because you aren't right

you blemish my heart
and leave me with bruises
that will never fade

so what do i do?
 because i can't stop
loving you

you hurt me

i don't want to sleep
because i don't want to wake up
and be the same person

i feel ugly, repulsive, disgusting
your words were like venom
and i spit them right back

hate is controlling me
and i don't want it to,
i don't want to be like this

i fear things will never
be okay with us,

i fear i really am the problem

the day i left

tears are forming in my eyes
because all i can think about
are my bare bedroom walls,
naked and dull
and how when i embraced you
and told you i loved you,
you didn't say it back

i will teach myself to swim

it feels like i'm standing
on the edge of a cliff
next to a calm sea
and at any moment
i could slip into the blue abyss

quietly, the water would
burden my lungs
and with my last breath,
i would whisper
"tomorrow will be better."

daydream

that summer, i watched you sing to the radio. i noticed that you bite your lip when you're trying to concentrate. i saw the glistening tears in your eyes before you quickly wiped them away. i believe that in those moments, i fell in love with your effortless, endearing manner. your careless actions captivated me. they made me want to sneak up behind you and plant a kiss on your cheek. i fell in love with you when you weren't looking.

i can't wait to meet you

sometimes i think about
how you woke up this morning
and brushed your teeth

i wonder how you like your coffee,
if you even like coffee at all,
and if you read the newspaper

why am i wasting my time
letting all these people
that don't really matter
break my heart?

when you're out there
somewhere
living your life and wondering
where i am

i know you're out there
and you're waiting for me too

talk is cheap

maybe
the most helpful thing
you could say
is not meant to be said
with words

please stay

i love you. i care.
i hate that you're so
f r a c t u r e d

i want to take care of you
i want you to be happy
and okay

tonight
you
b r o k e
my
heart

my entire body
shook with the fear
that you wouldn't be here
in the morning

i couldn't breathe
it felt as if
my lungs were being
c r u s h e d

why are you so sad?
i refuse to think of you
in the past tense

it's not your time
it's not your time
i t ' s   n o t   y o u r   t i m e

déjà vu

i don't cry about you anymore. my heart has grown numb to your name. you were mine, and now you're not. today, you're telling another girl your midnight secrets and turning her cheeks rosy with sweet melodic coos. i wonder if you play our song for her. i wonder if she notices how perfect you look when you're sleepy. i wonder if when you see her smile, you think of mine that's now fading. you've moved on, but i'm stuck in a swirling vortex of loving you. i only have myself to blame, because i had you, and then i lost you.

a n t

there are good types
of feeling small

like when you're in a big city
with tall buildings
and throngs of strangers
surrounding you,
painted with possibility

or when you're wrapped up
in someone's arms
and that person
feels so massive
and you feel so little
and protected
and safe

but this sensation
of small,
this feeling of
insignificance,
like an ant
that could be squished
and no one would care,

is not
a good feeling

flaws do not define you

although
the world is dirt,
i have seen
the most beautiful flowers
spring up
from its soil
(please do not pluck them all)

every rose has thorns,
but that shouldn't be a reason
to neglect its petals

e y e s

in my eyes
you'll read a mystery
with words so obscure
you'll have to use
a dictionary to understand

but when i look into yours,
it's like your mind has painted
those pools of blue
with all the words
you'll never say

that's why
you always
catch me
staring

m i d n i g h t

i don't want to be a rarity,
a full moon that only floats
in your midnight sky
once a month

nighttime feels so open,
you
shout things
you'd never whisper
in the daylight,
let go of the fear
that surfaces with the sun

i think i'll break all your clocks
at twelve in the morning
to immortalize
our honest midnights
so that your worries
will never rise

iii. haiku extended

you are my thoughts as
the sun rises, and my dreams
after it has set

it's been seven weeks
since you've said a word to me
the silence is void

i will love you still
after you've forgotten my
name, which will be soon

but if by chance i
cross your mind, tell me so and
never let me go

d e p t h

every individual
is so intricate,
yet we rush to peg them,
to label them,
to tell them who they are

if someone were to draw me,
i think they'd draw an outline
of my arms and legs
and form my lips
into a sweet smile

but if i were to draw myself,
i would darken the inner parts
of the outline with squiggles
and place a thousand different
expressions on my face

the more i meet people
and flip them inside out
to run my fingers along
the cracks of their beating heart,
the more i realize that
no one really is
"normal"

g o o d b y e

i should be glad
that you've moved on

that someone has filled
the spaces inside of you
i left vacant

that someone
will make you happy
in ways that i couldn't

that you're no longer
tormented by the aching
that i will never be yours

but i'm not
because i had a box
beneath my bed
in the shape of a heart
where yours was stored

i checked it today
and all that was left
was a note that read
"i now belong
to someone else"

n o r m a l

there once was a young girl with green eyes
who wore her soft blonde hair
in braided pigtails

at the age of seven,
she watched her older sister
stand in front of the mirror before school
and pinched her stomach with a disgusted face
neither of them ate breakfast that morning

at the age of nine,
she watched her older brother
make fun of a girl with glasses
for reading on the bus
she went home and hid all her books in the attic

at the age of twelve,
she watched the older girls at school
with straight hair and short skirts
put makeup on in the bathroom
and discuss how boys would only like you
if you looked perfect, like them
the next day she arrived with red lips, short shorts, and no
braided pigtails

at the age of fourteen,
she watched her father hit her mother for the first time
her mother cried when she saw her standing in the doorway
and told her he didn't mean it
the next year, she told herself that her boyfriend didn't mean
it either

at the age of sixteen,
she was paper thin and empty
with straight blonde hair, red lips,
bruised flesh, and lifeless green eyes
while staring at her reflection in the bathroom mirror, she
thought to herself, "at least i'm normal."

don't give up

i have felt the dizziness
that three words bring
and each time, they steal
away at the small collection of
faith i hold that promises
everything will eventually
be okay

"i give up," you tell me
with circles beneath
your eyes
and a heart
with a beat
that is nearing
the end
of a song

those words
are the words
that break me

because every day,
we're all trying our best
to keep it together
and when i see someone
pinned down to the ground
with the heaviness life brings,
i'm afraid i'll soon be
right there next to them

the lotus flower

you can either
keep yourself up at night
wondering
"why me?"
you can hide under your covers
and tell everyone
you're wrong and you'll
never be right

or you can see all this
heartbreak
pain
conflict
imperfection
as an opportunity
to emerge from the concealed depths
to the gleaming luminescence
and become stronger

it is your choice to decide
whether to drown in your troubles
or to courageously survive

because the harder the struggle
the more spirited you become in the end
"the deeper the mud
the more beautiful the lotus blooms."

p a t i e n c e

i never have to trim my nails
because of the anxiety that
has made itself at home
in the pit of my stomach

while tapping my feet,
i watch the clock slowly tick
and the breath in my lungs feels
thick and coated with doubt

but soon,
my time will come
and my eager feet
will carry me to a place where
hope fills my lungs and
i'll breathe with ease

because eventually,
everything is going
to work itself out

everything
will always be okay in the end
if you allow it to be

z a c h a r y

thank you
for introducing me
to good music

whenever i listen
to ernest greene
i think of you
and it's not sad,
it's not me missing you
or wishing things
were like they used to be

the thoughts
that are attached
to those songs
are happy
because i'm happy
i met you
even if now
we only speak
from time to time

you will always be
a happy memory

birthday eve

i feel trapped inside of my feverish skin
and i wish i could escape it,
because i don't want to be myself today

i don't know why i'm so different,
why i feel so lonely and tired of living

yesterday, i was so happy and hopeful,
inspired and alive
i lit candles and sang along to the radio
and grinned and felt completely intact
but today, i'm in pieces

i feel hollow and meaningless
i don't get why my feelings change so quickly

it's like once i've wrapped my arms
around them, the wind picks them up
and carries them away, leaving me
with a heart full of unfamiliar emotions
i don't understand
i just wish
i could figure myself out
sometimes

bad advice

keep your mind
on a tight leash
because if you let
your thoughts wander
they may end up in the clouds
where your hopes
are in the perfect position
to tragically fall

better off

no matter what i do,
i will never be good enough
for you

people tell me not to care,
that i just need to be tough,
but that isn't fair

because how do you stop caring?
it's not like pain
is a switch i can just turn off

you keep hurting me
and i need to learn that
maybe without you, i'm better off

b u l l y

before you let
a string of ignorant slurs
leave your malevolent lips

tell me about
how you've heard the thoughts
that inhabit my mind
and keep me up at night

tell me about
how you've felt the daily pain
that causes streams of salt water
to paint my cheeks

tell me about
all of my insecurities,
how while i'm good at loving others,
i don't know how to love myself

tell me about
everything i've gone through
and how hard i'm trying
to be strong

because if you still want to
tear me apart with your words
after you've considered all of that,
then perhaps you're the one
who needs help

see you soon

sometimes,
i get this weird sensation
where it feels like
i've known you forever

i miss you
even though
i've never had you
by my side

and i have these
pretend memories
of us together

they all seem so real,
even though
i know they're not

but hopefully
they will be,
one day

why pt. i

there's something
entrancing about you,
i hear melodies like honey
when you enter my mind

you make me smile
even when
the rain is falling
and i think i could
make you happy, too

the two of us together
could be as beautiful as
the setting sun

but of course
the wicked reality is
we'll never get
the chance

complimentative

the pages in my journal
do not hold enough space
for me to describe
in messy blue ink
how beautiful
you've made me feel
these past few days

rainy afternoons
are less gloomy
and the stars seem
so much easier to reach
from the cloud
you've put me on

i've been feeling
so much lighter
since i met you

u n t i t l e d

i'm the kind of girl
who leaves dying flowers on my desk
because i can still find beauty
in the withering petals

i hope you're the type of boy
who will remind me
to put water
in the vase

why pt. ii

when i asked you
why you're so sweet
and you replied

"because i like your smile,
you wear it so well
and if i can help with you smiling
then the world is a better place"

you stole the air from my lungs
in a pure and tragic manner

because one,
nobody
has ever been
so genuinely kind to me
i wish i could make you feel
as special as you make
me feel

and two,
i instantly thought
of my future
and it hurt my heart
because i'm almost certain
you won't be there

finally

i spent a lot of time
searching for affection
in shallow spaces

i gave people bits of me
they didn't deserve
and i let myself be hurt,
because i thought
that's what i deserved

but once i let go
of trying to shove puzzle pieces
in places they did not fit,
once i let go of all the hate
i secretly had stored in the
gashes that decorate my heart

i met you

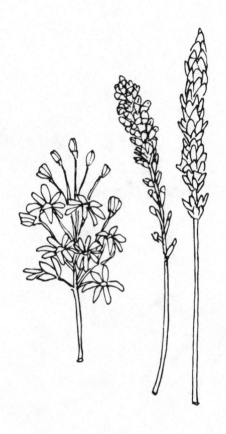

spring
2013

angel

i'm told that heaven
is a city made of gold
with pearly gates
and brilliant light,
but i couldn't care less
if it's crystal clear
or blanketed with fog

i just hope
heaven is a place
where i can kiss your soul,
capture a clip
of that radiant smile,
and play it back in the sky
forever

let go

i'm a scared little girl
with a low self esteem,
but i know You're there
standing right beside me

help me conquer
my countless fears
and allow You to wipe
my worry-filled tears

because holding on
to all my burdens
is such a heavy load

i know i need You,
i know i need
to just let go

you deserve the sun

i worry (a lot)
when i think (of other girls)
about how they (shine)
sparkle and radiate beauty
and about how i could be (brighter)

(and) nothing hurts worse than thinking about
not being with (you) my love, my heart
because i know you (deserve the) best,
you are my (sun), moon, and stars

insecurities

i want to ask you about your past,
but at the same time i don't
because my stomach becomes
more knotted than my hair
after a long, windy day at the beach
when thinking of a you
before me

i try to keep my mind from drifting
to the image of you holding her hand
and gazing into her eyes,
thinking about how her smile
is the reason
you smile

it hurts imagining
there was anyone before me
and i'm sorry,
because i know how unfair that is

i guess i'm just afraid
there was something in her
you'll notice is lacking
in me

you, you, you

it's a beautiful day today

my favorite weather
is when the sun
tenderly kisses my cheeks
and freckled shoulders

i see kids carelessly riding their bikes
and wind breezing
through the branches of tall trees
and i think of you

i think of how it would be
to lay in the middle of a soft green field
with our arms touching
and your hand holding mine

i wonder what animal you'd say
the clouds look like
and if you'd pick a flower
to place behind my ear
and look into my eyes
to tell me i'm more breathtaking
than any daisy
that has ever been quenched by summer rain

i think about you a lot,
and i know today
would be even more beautiful
with you by my side

same goes

some things
like rain in april
and popsicles on
the fourth of july
are meant to be

i hope the same goes
for you and me

my feelings woke me up

i've never known
something so fragile

i hold whatever this is
(you and i)
carefully,
with both hands

like glass,
it could shatter

the pieces
scattered

while i tiptoe
around the sharp fragments

trying to not let them
hurt me

like snow,
it melts

when the sun
comes up

to heat
the ground

and every time
i wish it'd stay

i hope my heart
will not become
like broken glass

i hope,
unlike snow
on a warm winter day,
you will decide
to never leave me

as deep as the ocean is between us

(as) i've begun to learn
who you are, and how (deep)
your soul is,
(as) i've begun to notice
how perfect you are for me,
each hour i long for (the) moment
where i may finally be by your side

like the blueness of the (ocean is) constant,
so are the thoughts (between) each second
that possess your name

i cannot think of a world
where an (us) does not exist
because i've become (so) attached
to the idea of always being yours

(is) it bad? is it good?
that (my) heart is forever set on you?
sometimes it's difficult to tell

i (love) days like today
when the sun is out
and my mind is clear like the sky,
i just wish you were here
to enjoy it

i will wait however long it takes
(for) that day to come
because i've never known anyone
as breathtaking as (you)

thank you

my heart
was in chains
my eyelids
heavy
my knees
weak

but You painted
my soul
with grace

You took my
burdens
and draped them
upon Yourself,
spread Your arms
wide
and said
"i love you
 this much"

You took my pain
You immersed me
in love
You continue
to guard my path

You
have set
me free

i promise to love every part of you

i want to take the bits of you i love
and press them like flowers
between the pages of my favorite book

and i want to take all the scraps
that you dislike in yourself
and display them on my refrigerator
to show you i'm still proud
of the person you are
and the person you are becoming

but most of all, i want to spin you like a globe
and drag my finger across till it stops
to discover the pieces of you
that you've yet to reveal to anyone else

i want to wrap them up in linen
and place them in an old cigar box,
i'd tuck it away safely
in the top drawer of my bedside table,
so you know i'll never let
those pieces of you go

because when you share
hidden parts of yourself
with someone else,
you're trusting that person
to hold the secret sections
of your heart
and to love the bits
you thought
were unlovable

more than words

i'm typically
good with words,
i can string them together
to create something similar
to when you look up and see sunlight
streaming through overhead trees
while standing in the middle of a dense forest

i'm typically good with words,
and i've strung plenty together about you,
but i'm getting to the point where the letters
are slowly disappearing
from the dictionary in my mind

you've taken my vocabulary
and jumbled it up
stealing x's and o's
and plenty of z's
replaced with late nights
thinking of what it'd be like
to place my hand on your chest
and feel your heart beat

p r a y e r

Lord,
i pray to You
with a heavy heart
and brittle bones

please let confidence
unfold like flowers
that sprout between my ribs

please take the butterflies
out of my stomach
because they crowd it
and make me sick

please fill my mind with the knowledge
that Your love is stronger than
all of the hate that fills the earth

please inscribe on my flesh
that You have a perfect plan for me,
and with You i can conquer
all of my doubts, all of my worries

please never let me forget
what You have done for me

please hold my hand
while on this wearisome journey
and allow me to find life in You

two in the morning

i think if we pressed our thumbs
on little ink pads
and left our fingerprints
on an unmarked page
side by side
they would look like
a lock and key
the swirls of mine
would fit perfectly in yours
much like i imagine
i would fit
in the comfort of your
arms

journal

i think the reason
we have such dark,
worrisome thoughts at night
is because the empty silence
found right before sleep
allows room for anxiety
to creep in and fill the spaces
between the floorboards
and peeling wallpaper
of our bedrooms

that may be why
when i haven't spoken to you
in awhile, i forget
all the good mornings
and five page letters
filled with words
that make my heart melt
like candle wax

i allow doubt to dwell in my soul,
along with thoughts
like how pitiful it is
for me to be vacant
because you're not here
to occupy my confidence
and reassure me that
time nor interval
will change
how you feel

maxwell

his heart was full of depth,
but he chose to let it hide
and masked his pain with pills
and smokes and jokes and lies

i'll never forget you,
i'll never regret you

i didn't know it was possible
to lay in bed shaking with sorrow a
nd still be able to genuinely smile
through the silent tears falling down my face

my eyes were finally opened
to what honest-to-goodness love is
when i knew i couldn't be selfish with you,
because although my bones ache for us to work,
i want to put your heart before mine

it's difficult coming to the realization
that you're just a step in the right direction
and not my journey's end

you'd expect this to hurt
and it does,
i'm still wiping away
the sadness from my eyes

but it's okay,
the hurting is helping
because i know i grow in pain

there's no doubt in my mind
that you loved me with your whole heart,
you painted a picture on my soul
that depicts how i deserve to be treated

i'm not bitter
because i know through all of this
i'm coming out better

false ending

instead of pursuing the difficult,
yet beautiful bundle of perfection
we once held, you and i chose
to fall apart and plunge into separate depths

although you've decided to run north
while i'm patiently waiting in the east
for this torment to run its course,
i know that our love
was real and true and pure

love is selfless and kind,
and whilst i wish i could grab your hand
and beg you to never let me go,
i'm allowing the pain that comes with love lost
to scrape my heart and strengthen my soul

my eyes are set on heavenly things
and captivated by an eternal outlook:
i know i am becoming stronger
so that i may have more endurance
for future suffering

i know you didn't give up on me
nor did i give up on you,
instead i'm choosing to love you
by letting you go

which hurts worse

which hurts worse?

a beautiful person
who treated you like gold
deciding it's best for the two of you
to go your separate ways,
it just won't work
(even though "i love you endlessly")

or

someone
who pretended to care
telling you (after you poured yourself out to them)
"my feelings for you are gone,"
or were never even there at all

tuesday evening thoughts

i have a consuming desire to know everyone

when i peer out of the car window
and look upwards to see a plane
leaving a vapor trail across the pink
and purple blended sky,
i can't help but let my mind bloom
with thoughts of who is up there

i wish i could go through the aisles,
sit down next to each passenger,
and watch their eyes light up
or become watery, or both,
as they tell me their story

i want to know
where they're going
where they're coming from
i want to know
their favorite moments
what cheers them up on bad days
their thoughts before sleep
what their "one day" dreams are
i want to know
what puts a smile on their face
and what breaks their heart

i want to know them inside and out
because i fully believe
that at the core of each individual
there is beauty

some choose to let it radiate outwardly,
some are too afraid to let it shine

so many people don't know they're beautiful,
and maybe that's the reason
i wish i could cross paths with the whole world

i wish i could show everyone
how beautiful they truly are

carry on

your words were so lovely
that i never once doubted them,
i couldn't hear the emptiness
or read into the sugar coated lies
masquerading as sincere promises

i wrote them in cursive
and dotted the i's with little hearts,
counting on the vows to hold weight

but when i finally tested them
by throwing your forevers into the ocean,
they did not sink to the bottom,
instead they floated right on the surface

your guarantees
were like funhouse mirrors,
i ran in one direction
thinking it was leading me
to where i needed to be,
but i came to a dead end,
trapped and brokenhearted
with your voice echoing somewhere
"i cannot mend it"

i will not let my journal
turn into pitiful pages
filled with only your name

i will carry on,
bruised by your half-truths
and with eyes full of hope,
nevertheless

you will always be good enough

if you feel unsatisfied
with who (you) are,
destroy the bits
you don't like in yourself,
(will) yourself to keep fighting,
because there is (always)
a chance to make things better
instead of completely destroying
who you could (be)

"(good) things come
to those who wait,"
but sometimes time is
not (enough) to cure the
overwhelming aching feeling
that keeps you in bed
on sunny days

you have to fight to be alright

it may not be easy,
but it's worth it

so look at all of the weight the world holds
that's waiting for its chance to crush you,
and say "today, i am going to be okay."

black and white

if you're laying in bed
wrapped up in sheets
of miserable thought,
go to sleep

if thumbing through old messages
only causes your heart to ache
and long for something unattainable
erase them

if it hurts to keep
everything you're feeling
bottled up inside
let it out

if you're clinging onto someone
that doesn't treat you like
you're worth the world
let them go

because sometimes
we choose to believe
that things are only
indistinguishable shades of grey
when in reality,
life is more black and white
than it seems

if you're unhappy
with the way
you are living your life
change it

r e a l

even with my heart
broken into
seven hundred
sixty-four thousand pieces,
somehow i still manage
to love you

n o s t a l g i c

i love you
i love you
i love you
and i'll never stop loving you,
i couldn't even if i tried

you've taken all of me,
scrubbed the dirt from my flesh
and replaced it with rose petals
and i love you, i love you, i love you

thank you for making me feel beautiful
for the first time in a long time

searching

life is full of *searching*

searching for someone who appreciates you,
who understands each deep thought
that fills your mind and holds your hand
even when those thoughts are unclear

we *search* for light in dark places,
hoping that things aren't truly as
grim as they appear to be

we *search* for time and consequently
waste it in the process

so often we spend days and months
and years *searching* for something
we think will steady our hearts

step back and take a moment
to inhale and exhale with eyes closed,
and the one thing that will bring forth
pure joy will become clear, it will
stand out and beckon for your attention

you then have a choice:
either pretend you can find a light
more satisfying and continue to search
blindly for something that will never appear,
or look at the love and hope you've found,
and put your faith and trust in the
most brilliant light you'll ever see

why would you keep *searching*
for stars in the shadows
when there's already a sun shining
in your sky?

j o y

it's when
your heart is full
and smiling
when life tries to
chip your happiness away
and it's courage
when fear tries to
take ahold of your direction
and it's peace
when nothing in your
life is stable
and it is love in your bones
when the rest of the
world is telling you no

part i: thoughts before sleep

how do you expect me
to believe i deserve better
when you're the one proving
that i'm not worth fighting for

and don't you even dare say
"it's not you, it's me"
because i know one day
you will meet a girl
and her eyes will shine like diamonds
and your heart will always
ache to be next to her
and you will do whatever it takes
to have her, no matter what
you will overcome every obstacle
to ensure that she is forever yours

so don't even try to feed me lies like
"you are good enough"
when you're completely contradicting that
by leaving me here broken and alone

part ii: thoughts with a clear mind

thirty-eight days
twenty poems
and an embarrassing amount
of doodled hearts later,
the reality of you not being my one
has finally begun to set in

it's been one week
of trying to get over you
and i still cried last night
and i will probably cry again
but not forever
because i know that i know that i know
that i deserve so much better

i deserve
someone who will think
my eyes shine like diamonds
and whose heart will always
ache to be next to me
and who will do whatever it takes
to have me, no matter what
someone who will overcome every obstacle
to ensure that i am forever his

and this will be
my last poem about you
and tomorrow will be day one
of erasing your name from my heart
 and it's going to sting
because i really was hoping
you'd stay

but no,
i now see that you
are not my one

you are only one step
in the right direction

h o p e

hope is beautiful
and can be destructive
at the same time
it keeps us hanging on,
but sometimes
for things
that will never come

am i the only one

i don't always like
contentment and simplicity

because i love waking up smiling
and falling asleep smiling
and the feeling of my heart racing
from the onset of a new adventure

and loss and pain
can be just as exhilarating
because while it hurts,
there's still an opened door
somewhere
that promises hope
of a better future

so when i'm not immersed
in a beginning or an ending
and i'm stuck in the middle
of monotonous emptiness,
i am at risk of throwing myself
into avoidable heartbreak

just to feel something,
anything at all

genie

i asked
what you would wish for
if a genie
granted you three wishes

and none of your wishes
had anything to do
with me

i wish i could carry your burdens

you are bright eyes
masking grey storm clouds
in your mind
and a heart too big
for the cavity of sadness
that confines it

and you are a bird
trying so desperately
to keep flying
in the pouring rain

i am the hands
that long to caress your gentle face
and an autumn breeze
seeking to whisk away
your worries

and i am just a girl
praying for a thunderstorm
so that you may have
endless clear skies

w e

often, i picture us
holding hands and watching movies
sitting on benches beneath old oak trees
hearing your laugh throughout the day
and catching you smile
when you think i don't see

and all i can do is hope
that when you close your eyes
your mind is filled
with thoughts of me

late night phone calls

tonight i miss you
more than usual
because i'm thinking
of all the times we stayed up late
and whispered hello to each other
through the darkness and crackling phone line
and i had to stifle my giggles
beneath the covers

eventually we'd both grow tired
and you'd sing me to rest

listening to your voice
while i fell asleep
was the closest i'd ever come to happiness
your melodies echoed through
my dreams and they still bounce
off my walls on nights like these

bucket list worthy

there is something
inexpressibly beautiful
about the world
  when the sun begins to rise
and fill the dim sky
with soft rays of light
  and only the birds are awake
to sing to you "good morning"
while everyone else
  is curled up in their beds
unaware of the magnificence
they're missing
  and everything feels so simple
it's as if six a.m. is an epiphany
that sparks at your fingertips
  and spreads until
you are encompassed entirely
by a feeling of clarity
  there is something
inexpressibly beautiful
about being awake to behold
  the splendor of this world
while everyone else
is still asleep

augustus

i know i am young,
i know i am only seventeen,
but when i think of him
and his incandescent smile,
my heart swells and beats in time
with the cadence of his alluring words

his mind is like no other,
filled with such deep
and captivating thoughts
that flutter from place to place
like a moth, and like a moth
i am drawn to his brilliance

i long to hold his face in my hands
and trace his lips with my fingertips
and when i close my eyes
all i see is the way he looks at me,
as if i'm the one who paints
the summer evening sky

i know i am young,
i know i am only seventeen,
but i think i could spend
the rest of my life searching
and never find anything
nearly as beautiful as
the way he loves me

summer

you told me
  you were going to change
to be a better you for me
  and you said you wanted
so badly to make this work

i gave you every bit of me
  and you tried to give me
every bit of you, but
  it was too difficult
for you to try to love yourself
  when you were giving
so much of yourself to me

before i didn't want to let go,
  i wanted to keep believing that
  maybe
you'd be able to love me
as much as i loved you

and now that i've let go,
it doesn't feel like you're gone
  more so, it feels like i'm the one
  who has left you standing
  with your face in your hands,
wishing you'd been able to be
a better you for me

i don't doubt that one day
  you'll be an amazing you
for someone else
  and that one day
it'll all make sense to both of us

and i don't doubt
  that one day
i will find someone
who will love me
as much as you wanted to

favor unreturned

she was like
        a wilting flower
drained of all things
that kept the others upright

he was like
        a rushing brook
who saw her crumpled and tired,
crowded by overgrown weeds,
and wanted nothing more
than to clear the earth around her
and see her bloom again

so he took all he had
        and poured it into her
and when finally the pinkness
had returned to her cheeks
        she looked back at him
        and saw that

he was now like
        a withering shrub
frail and planted in dry clay

and despite the deep conviction
she had in her heart to restore him
        like he had restored her
all of her best efforts
left her with with exposed roots
and dirt beneath her fingernails

he wouldn't let her stay
        to continue to try
        to quench his thirst
so she left him with a watering can
and promised he'd soon find relief

it seems

your name is always
on the tip of my tongue
and if you
wrap me in a blanket
and place me by the fire,
in the flames
i'll see your smile,
but if i blink
it'll disappear
because our time
while full, was fleeting
and now you are just
dandelion seeds
in the summer breeze
that will land
in another yard
to make someone else's
wishes come true

today

the thing about feelings
is that they change
yesterday,
  you may have been
   completely infatuated
    with someone
     or entirely immersed
     in sadness,
   but that doesn't mean
that's how you feel now
or how you'll feel forever
and i fear that people forget that,
  i fear we fail to remember
   that emotions are not permanent
    and maybe that's why
     her stomach hurts
    when she thinks about
   the girls in his life
before her
or why i'm reluctant
  to share old poems
   because i don't want anyone
    to think that's how i feel today
    so maybe we should start asking
"how are you?" more often
  and stop accepting
   the default "i'm okay."
    and maybe we should start
   caring more about
  what people say now,
 instead of dwelling on
words of the past

chasing light

currently i am not
   sad
     depressed
        lonely
  alone
   self-loathing
      insecure
 heartbroken
   nor breaking hearts
and that makes me feel quite
  out of
            place
because i am surrounded by scars
   and tear-streaked (beautiful) faces
  bruised knees drawn up to chests
   dark empty rooms
  broken mirrors
   and trashcans filled
  with crumpled lists of mistakes
and if i could,
i would take all the
  scars
   tears
   and lonely nights
from the hearts that are broken
          or breaking
and i wish i could
 cloak The Light i've found
  (or did It find me?)
   around cold shoulders
and wash all the tired feet
  that've been blindly stumbling
   in the dark

summer
2013

speechless

i wish we could go to a park at night and sit back to back
on a blanket beneath the trees
and talk until the stars tell us to go home because when i
look at you straight on
my knees grow weak and my voice shakes and maybe i'm
not exactly sure what to say when i'm distracted by
all the what ifs in your eyes
and maybe my mind dizzies with thought like the possibility
that i could be
a high tidal wave
that washes away the foundations of a barely built sandcastle
and maybe i just wish i could tell you everything on my
mind at 2am
and maybe i'm just really hoping you feel the same way

cliché

you caught my eye
when i usually barely glance
and i know it was for a reason
because i don't really
believe in "chance"

and you told me
the day you saw me
you noticed
there was something
different about me, too

so i hope you remember
to not treat like like
just another girl

andrea

although you've gotten taller,
your eyes have remained
the same shade of trusting brown
and deep down
you are still the little girl
who stayed up late
whispering secrets to her best friend
beneath flower patterned sheets

and you're still afraid of spiders
and you still cannot sit still
and as you grew up
you noticed that the world
is a lot smaller than it used to seem

and i think when you looked
into the wonder-filled eyes
of this little girl
you saw a reflection of yourself
and it reminded you that
although you've gotten taller,
your eyes have retained
that same glimmer of hope

my time will come

i'm beginning to realize
that i go into a situation
thinking things
are going to go
a certain way,
and i get my hopes up
and i pray that everything
will go according to plan,
but then later on
it's brought to my attention
that God didn't put me
in that place
to be blessed,
but to bless
someone else

and i guess it can get
a little disappointing,
because i start to feel
a little empty-handed,
but it's also comforting
knowing that God is using me
because He knows
i'm strong enough
to do His work

paper cranes

you told me
to write down my feelings
and share them with you
when you wake up,
but drawing out these emotions
isn't easy because
they're pale and indefinite

i cannot distinguish
a path to take,
whether it's winding
or cobblestoned,
or so overgrown with trees
that i cannot see the sky

so maybe in the meantime
i'll sit in my room
and fold paper cranes
on rainy days
till a map that illustrates
how to carry on
makes its way
into my muddled hands

hindsight bias

looking back, i've realized
that in the moment
i tend to be anxious and impatient
and i don't trust
that everything will work itself out
and i ache to know
exactly what is waiting for me
around the corner
> will i alter my circumstances
> or will my circumstances alter me?

i mindlessly allow myself to become faithless
and although i've overcome so many obstacles,
my eyes become fixated on the present
and i forget to take a step back
and reflect on my past

everyone always says,
"don't look back,"
but i think it's important
to remember where you once stood
and recognize how far you've come

i know i've changed
and i know i will continue to change

so why at 2am on a monday night
do i get stuck believing
that things will always be the same?

love, jesus

darling girl,
why do you cry yourself to sleep every night
praying for someone
to come along and give you love,
to stay up with you till three in the morning
and listen attentively
as you list off all of your
passions, worries, burdens
to be envious of your attention
to kiss your forehead
and hold you without judgment
to be there for you
when you feel alone
to assure you everything will be okay
and remind you
that every sunrise and crashing wave
is a chance to make things right

when I'm right here
waiting for you with open arms,
ready to replenish
every empty space in your heart
because although you're imperfect
and you hate the way
your front tooth is slightly crooked

I see you perfectly

darling girl,
why haven't you opened your eyes to realize
that I've been here for you
all along

my advice

1. *don't be afraid of getting hurt*
because in life there are times
when we need to be vulnerable
an unmatchable brilliance is radiated
when you bare your soul to another
and are privileged enough to be shown
the deepest parts of their spirit in return

2. *write often*
no one has to see it, you can scribble
on napkins and throw them away
but please, allow yourself to know
the freedom of letting words seep
from your heart and relieving
the heavy strain of carrying
so many smothering thoughts

3. *never promise forever*
because not once have i met
a person whose forever lasted
and i can't say
i remember a time
when my forever has lasted, either

fiction

no word is strong
yet gentle enough
to convey what i feel
for you

you hold so much back
while i pour out my heart

i want to go back
and live in the moments
when you looked at me
with loving eyes

now all i see
is pain radiating
from your careful soul

all i've done
is stolen a couple beats from your heart
and left you in an ocean of guilt
for breaking mine

f o r g o t t e n

soon i will f a d e
like a photograph
left upon the windowsill,
and you will wipe away
my name from your lips

my laughter will become
a faintly familiar echo
in the hollows of your memory,
and unlike your thriving soul,
i will be fixed in a state of affliction
by the absence of your tenderness

yes, the fire in your heart
that once burned brightly for me
is growing dimmer by the hour,
however, you shall remain with me
a l w a y s

m o r n i n g

there are
so many meadows
i have not
so many roads
i have not
so many mountains
i have not
so many songs
i have not
so many books
i have not
so many hearts
i have not

so many
i have not

so many
i have

so many
i forget
so many
i do not see

hold on

you get to a point where it starts to feel okay to feel again, and the midnight air doesn't suffocate you, and the sky doesn't seem to hang so low anymore, and if i would've told myself this a month ago, that it'd all be okay, i wouldn't have believed it, but here i am, standing in the middle of a forest with no one around for miles and miles, and i do not feel alone.

j u g g l e

you told me to take up new hobbies
to distract myself from the pain
you were causing me

you told me to learn origami
so i did
and now my room is crowded
by paper cranes folded each time
your name came to mind

and you told me
to learn how to juggle
so i did,
but not in the way
you were talking about

inevitable

if you told my heart to beat
it would
but not because you told it to
and if you told me to love you
i would
but not because you told me to

i'm hurting

you have hurt me,
you are hurting me,
you will hurt me

there have been
so many headaches and heartaches
because of you,
so many lost breaths
because of you,
so many nights spent
crying on my cold bedroom floor
because of you

but i will love you,
i love you,
i have always loved you

remember me

i feel as though i am easily forgotten,
attention held shortly
adored briefly
brushed aside thoughtlessly
a fleeting memory

but i remember half birthdays
and strangers' sleepy smiles
on the crowded sidewalk this morning

i remember
when you told me that
color is like music
and you see most things
in shades of blue

i am faded print,
you are underlined and circled

i am simple similes,
you are intricate analogies

you close your eyes and a couple stars
illuminate the darkness,
i close my eyes and see infinite galaxies

your wandering thoughts have abandoned me

four in the morning

I'm going through withdrawals. How awful it is to have to keep yourself from speaking to someone because you know if they wanted to speak to you, they would. I'm so deeply rooted in the sand that no waves that crash on land could overturn me. Your footprints are leading away from me, you are moving further and further down the shoreline, your outline growing smaller, smaller, smaller, blending in with the horizon where the sun is setting in lovely shades of red. I do not fear that you will not be loved, because even now I see how the birds adoringly sing your name. I fear the drops of saltwater that fall down my face each solemn night will one day be able to collect into ocean of their own. I fear the birds will be able to love you better than I have. I fear that this titanic amount of heaviness weighing on my heart will be ever-present. Your name is written in the clouds, and I cannot escape it, for no matter how far I run, I can never escape the sky. When I look up, there it is, and so are you.

i don't want to let go

all of the words
you speak
today and tomorrow
are in vain

for you do not wish
to throw rocks at my window,
you know very well
i am already on my doorstep
waiting for you

you love me in songs played
on tuesday afternoons,
gaps in conversation where
three words are meant to fill it
and faded journal entries
dated when time was blind

you've written disguised goodbyes
beneath my eyes
and subliminally (explicitly)
whispered (shouted)
to move on, move on, move on
each moment i've tried to draw you nearer,
you do your best to push me further away

but even from a distance,
you are still holding on

let me go
let me go
let me go

so i may finally
let go
of
you

m e l a t o n i n

tonight,
i will lay my head on my pillow
and my mind will be silent
and i don't know if that's
better or worse than
a thousand disarrayed thoughts
keeping me awake,
because regardless of
whether or not
i'm thinking of you
and wondering if
you're thinking of me,
whether or not
i'm thinking of this
or that or anything
that makes me feel,
it still takes forever
to fall asleep

does time truly heal all wounds?

I will not ask you to stay

If you must go, go
I don't need you
I will breathe (carefully) without you
I will smile (slowly) without you
I will go on (eventually) without you

I'd be much happier
If you chose to not leave,
But if you must let go, let go
And I will too

Hopefully one day
I will teach my heart to not break
Whenever everyday thoughts
Lead to you

I'm afraid I'm much too weak,
I'm afraid we'll always be
A book with the end pages ripped out,
I'm afraid I'll always wonder,
Always ache,
Always place everyone second to you

I'm afraid I'll always love you,
But I will not ask you to stay

so very alone

Am I really so alone in my own thought
That I can find no one with the same vision as me?
The same astonishment?
The same confusion?
The same frustration?
Someone who may console me
And tell me that I am not insane?
Am I insane?
If I am not, then why can't I find a single soul that
See things the way I see them?
Is everyone blind?
Am I?

God is my favorite artist, salvation is my favorite song

My breath is lost as I gaze upon the magnitude of the mountains that surround me. I marvel at how beautifully the water reflects the sky, pure white clouds stretched across blankets of soft pinks and blues as the sun sets behind the trees. I see the steadiness of Your hand in the horizon. I see Your love of variety in shells scattered along the shoreline. I see Your flawless detail in the veins of a maple leaf. I see Your creative spark in fireflies glowing subtly against the darkness of an airy August night. I hear You in the winter wind, I feel You in the summer heat. My soul is flooded with joy at the sight of Your creation. I cannot help but lift my hands and praise You.

a u s t r a l i a

A part of me lives miles and minutes and moments away
in an indefinite, dreamy place
where clocks are not my enemy
and I associate the word "distance" with travel, not longing

My heart has sailed across the Atlantic,
moved eagerly through the Indian Ocean,
navigated using an atlas inked with butterflies
and stars that gleam ardently
(just as your rosemary eyes do,
every once in a blue moon,
when you're able to sew together
the disarrayed thoughts
that dwell in your messy head)

You are so, so far away

However, if I avoid calendars and geography,
it feels like you're right here beside me

In the afternoon, when the sun shines
through my bedroom window
and paints the world map on my wall with light,
I shut my eyelids and run my thumb along the string
that stretches across the parchment,
connecting me to you

I pretend that when I open my eyes,
you will be here
and that my aching fingers
that are so desperately
grasping the paper
will be intertwined
with yours

d u s t

I feel invisible
Yet you claim(ed) I am the air you breathe
And perhaps like air I am always present,
But presently forgotten

The heaviness of your hush is crushing me with empty blows
This silence leads me to wander down a path cloaked in a
heavy mist
That whispers harsh truths such as:
Our hopeless, fictitious, drawn out infatuation is like
A library book that was checked out last March
You underlined and doggie-paged the first few chapters and
Then left it on your shelf to collect dust all of April and May

I foolishly kept begging you to finish the book
Read the last sentence
Take time to skim over the epilogue
Please
Find your way to the back cover

I foolishly ignored your "I can't"s

And now it's late August and our love is long overdue,
In the opposite sense of what the phrase typically means

I write with angry lead because
I am too stubborn to admit
I just filled a trash bin with tissues
And that the cuffed sleeves of my flannel
Are damp like grass's morning dew

I have so much more to say,
Although I cannot find the words
To say anything more than

You should've written.

Because two weeks of nothing
Was enough for me to realize
That you are just a passing breeze
Seldom present, presently becoming something of the past

goodnight or goodbye?

The air feels like falling action,
It feels like this is coming to an end
I can see the curtains closing
And I don't know why I haven't cried or
Why my heart feels like it's made of stone

Maybe this isn't the end!
Maybe it's a new chapter!
A rising sun!
A see you soon!
(How should I know to say goodnight and not goodbye?)

But if this does end
If it's a closed book
A setting sun
Never see you again
(How should I know to say goodbye and not goodnight?)

I know we tried,
I know we loved with full hearts,
I know it hurts to say goodbye

don't forget to live

Time isn't wasted at the end of the day
When you're in bed thinking about all the things
You could've done,
You could've said,
All the empty boxes left on your to do list

Time is wasted
When you're standing on a rock at the edge of a waterhole
And decide to not jump
When you're sitting in your car
Trying to justify reasons for not going in
When you anxiously hit backspace
Instead of expressing how you truly feel
When you ignore your heart that's screaming
"You deserve better."

It's lost in I could have and I should have,
In missed opportunities,
In letting fears override judgment

Time is not necessarily wasted
In passing minutes, months, years
We waste time by
Counting seconds,
And by letting seconds pass
When we could've made
Those seconds count

i'd rather have a lovely heart than a lovely face

I'd rather have scars on my cheeks
And a crooked nose and
Bad skin and boney hips
Or boring eyes and boring hair and a boring mouth
And someone tell me
"You're beautiful,"

Because I'd know they meant
I am beautiful in the way that I talk,
In the way that I listen, in the way that I love,
In the way that I am

Than have

Pretty lips and pretty teeth and
Pretty hair and a pretty nose
And ignorantly believe
That being beautiful in the way that I look
Is enough

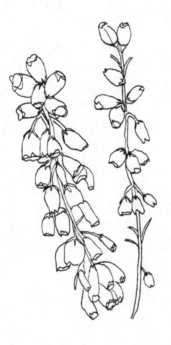

autumn & winter
2013

b r e a t h e

Don't forget to get away every once in awhile,
To lose yourself in a book
Or in the woods behind your home

Ride your bike into the sunset,
Sit on your front steps and count the cars passing by,
Lay on your roof and gaze up at the night sky,
Drive along back roads with the windows rolled down
Listening to nothing but the sound of rushing wind

I hope you take the time to be alone,
To sort through the cluttered shelves of your heart

I hope you take the time to be silent,
To close your eyes and just listen

I hope you take the time to be still,
To quiet your mind and experience the beauty
Of simply Being

today i learned how to fly

I'm afraid to write about you because
Ink makes me feel everything,
And everything feels so much more real
When my cursive words smudge up against
The side of my hand and stain it blue
As my pen races to keep up with my heart

But it can't be real,
Because I thought I was moving on,
I thought I was growing up,
I thought I knew all of this was
Foolish and starry-eyed

I thought, I thought, I thought
But maybe I need to stop thinking
And just let myself feel;
Feel the butterflies you put in my stomach,
Feel the pure bliss you infuse into my bloodstream

And maybe I don't need to know everything,
Like exactly what you're thinking
Or exactly how I feel
Or how all of this is going to turn out

I guess what I'm saying is that
Everything isn't always going to be clear,
I may come up to two roads
And not be absolutely certain which one
I'm meant to take,
But I do know that whichever path I choose,
I'd like to be able to scan the trees and smile
Because you're there walking alongside me

thirty-six hours of silence

I don't have a problem with saying too little, you don't have to carve inspiration into a health room desk or vandalize a bathroom stall to get me to tell him how I feel. I have a problem with acting as if it's four a.m. all day long and forgetting that you don't need to know about my every mood swing: my Sunday highs and Tuesdays lows and Thursday nothings. I think my biggest fault is bothering you to tell me all the thoughts that have yet to cross your mind (and maybe wishing they had.) I want you to want to know everything I feel at any given moment: what I thought of this evening's sunset and how long it took me to fall asleep last night and why track two of my favorite album makes me feel like I'm in a dream. I want you to want me to know why you painted your bedroom walls yellow and how often you floss your teeth and which day of the week you feel happiest on. But most of all, I want to know everything you feel, even before you've felt it.

seventeenth

Here's something you seldom hear: don't always listen to your heart. Because if your heart is like mine, it's often fickle and confused. Emotions aren't always true, they may come and go with the wind. Feelings trick us into believing lies. You look in the mirror and feel inadequate. You hear something so many times that you start to believe it's true. You take a situation and manipulate it till it's something completely false. But it's time you start listening to your head: you may not be in control of what you feel, but you are in control of how you handle those feelings. Look in the mirror and tell yourself, "I know I am beautiful." Refuse to believe the lies. Remind yourself of your many wonderful qualities. Don't read too far into things, take them as they are. Worrying doesn't change tomorrow, it just makes today more troublesome. Decide to be happy. Decide to be okay. Don't believe everything you feel.

you are with me

the scent of incense mixed with rain is diluting the redolence of missing you, but no matter how many stormy nights i spend reading and listening and trying to find contentment in silence and simplicity, i will forever see your name between every line, hear your voice in every song, feel the absence of your presence in every moment spent alone. you are with me, you are with me, you are with me. you are always with me.

the end

here i am
sitting at my typewriter
as tears trickle down my cheeks
and i can hardly breathe
because i know it's over
and that this isn't just another
false ending
it's really, truly over
and i hate that you had to hear my voice quiver
i just pray you'll be happy
and that everything will work out for you
in the end
you are so special
you are so special
you are so special
i will miss you forever
but i don't doubt that i'll see you again
in that distant place
i know that all will be well
and we won't think of the pain
or the hurt
or the fights
or the tears
we'll just be thankful for all the goodness
that came from two hearts
being so vulnerable with each other
everything will be okay
i'll be okay
please do not worry
you are good
i don't blame you
i know i'll be okay
i just wish i could've been okay
with you
this hurts so much
but it won't hurt forever

goodbye

p.s. i forgive you

imaginary

I'm standing here, thinking of you, while the
wind blows through my hair and the sea creeps
ashore to kiss my toes. The scent of salty
ocean air is soothing, but the ache of
missing you lingers still. I can see the
sun setting in the distance. The soft
oranges and yellows remind me that endings
can be beautiful, no matter how much I
wish the sun would stay just a little while
longer. As the sky begins to fade to a
somber shade of blue, I close my eyes and
allow my mind to focus on the white
noise of crashing waves, praying
that when I open them, the sun will have
risen, and you will be standing here beside me

i'll hug you next time i see you

I know it hurts like heavy nothingness, and it feels like everything was pointless. Like it was all wasted time and effort and feelings, avoidable heartache, disposable passion. I know it hurts, and you're hoping it's all a lie, that you'll close your eyes and everything will go back to the way it used to be. But even though it feels impossible now, you will learn to let go. It may take awhile, and it may always sting, but one thing that's certain is that you will be okay. You'll learn to breathe again without wincing, you won't flinch at the sound of her name. First it'll be a day, then two, then weeks and months and you'll forget all about the pain. You'll smile and laugh and it won't be fleeting or fake, it'll be real. You are going to be happy again. I know it hurts. I know. It's okay that it hurts, you're human. But I promise you, it won't hurt forever.

writing advice

write from your heart: scribble down words
when you're crying at 2am, or right after
you've gotten home from spending time with
someone you love, whenever your emotions
are at their peak. writing is best when it's
pure and raw and genuine. don't filter when you
write, just let your soul flow out onto the page

i am me

i am
monday nights filled with
candlelit journal entries
and sipping hot tea while
watching rain bounce off
the roof and open windows
in autumn and messy hand-
written letters and white
tees and cuffed jeans and
pb&j with the crust cut
off and folded origami
cranes and watching the
sun rise while everyone
else is tucked away in
their beds and midnight
car rides and candid smiles
and lists written in blue
ink and wildflowers and
mountains and birds singing
and books and movies that
make you cry and nicknames
and flannels in the winter
and soft music and loud
music and moments recorded
only by memory and pumpkin
pie and forever stamps
i am all the little things
and if you don't make an
effort to understand why i
love all the things i love
you will never understand
me

m e m o r i e s

it's strange to think
you will only remember me
as the person i was with you

you'll never learn of my new habits,
nor will i ever come to know yours
i won't get to watch you grow,
see you become strong,
hear about all of your new
adventures and revelations

no, i am only left
with who you were

we're both frozen in time
in each others' memories

u n e a s y

my heart doesn't feel things the same way it used to. i feel so… that feeling you get when you take a photo with someone you don't know very well and you're unsure if you should put an arm around them or not. i used to *feel everything all at once,* now i just feel… stagnant. no tragedy, no infatuation, i'm over you, i'm moving on, i'm not drowning in any sea of emotion. i'm stranded in an apathetic desert. i need *something. anything.* captivate me, break my heart, i don't like this silence.

give me something to write about.

not that you asked

i wish i could peel up the floorboards
and lie beneath them
there i could hide in still silence,
but it still wouldn't be completely
silent because i cannot leave my
mind behind

i couldn't tell you what i'm thinking*
even if i wanted to
i thought that i had words for
everything, that i could always find
refuge in my ability to arrange
letters into feeling

i can't

this emotion is a lightning bolt
and i am a bare tree alone
in a barren field

*what's the difference between
thinking and feeling? how do you know
if it's coming from the
head or the heart?

the healing process

no use in wondering if you saved my letters
or still look at photographs of me and sigh
because at the end of the day
when i'm wrapped up in sheets and blankets
wearing wooly socks and thick leggings and flannel
i'm still cold
and you're still
so far away
in so many ways
and i miss you, i miss you, i miss you
i miss you
but i can't tell you
and i won't tell you
because even if you miss me
like i miss you
i'm the one
who tripped up the stairs
and even if you offered me a hand
(you didn't, that's okay)
i couldn't take it
because i need to clean
the cuts on my knees
and wait for the bruises to fade
on my own
so while it seems that you're fine now
with taking the stairs two at a time,
i'm still trying
to stand on my feet
and i miss you, i miss you, i miss you
i really freaking miss you
and i'm trying so hard
to be strong

a d v e n t u r e

i find myself
staring out waiting room
windows,
my eyes follow the footsteps
of the strangers below
as i dream about being apart
of their everyday monotony,
because what may be a
dully, normal, tasteless
indifferent thursday to them
would be an adventure
to me

written on leaves

curled up beneath the duvet
knees drawn up to chest
inhaling the smoky scent of my fleece
sewn fresh nostalgia
I remembered how
we laughed and ate off chinaware
while sipping out of plastic cups
sitting by the fire pit
in the backyard
my eyes wandered
towards the woods at dusk
and I breathed
realizing we are just specks of dust
that glimmer in the light of our creator

f a l l

i wasn't feeling okay
so i put on my overalls and went
outside
to wander around my backyard,
trekking around in clunky rain boots
as i hummed and tried not to think
i like to write little notes
on the leaves that are now
changing colors
and when i'm done
i let them
fall
so i can flatten them
beneath my heel
till the small words
are crinkled and no longer legible
amongst the dirt and grass
and so desperately,
i wish i could
let the thoughts in my head
fall
to the ground
so i could flatten
these pitiful feelings
beneath my heel
until they were no longer legible
amongst the hurt and hopefulness
in my heart

every day is a victory

just as you cannot stare at a cut
and watch it heal,
you can't keep glaring at the pain
and expect it to go away

so look away

let your eyes focus on
daily beauties like sun that shines
through bedroom blinds
and warm sheets
that wrap you up at night

saturday mornings
and crisp november air,
hot showers and the Opportunity
that waits for you at your front step
each and every morning

and one day,
you'll unravel the bandage
you've wrapped around your heart
and the only thing you'll see is a light scar
that's there to remind you
of how strong you've become

although this life is beautiful,
it isn't easy
and whether you believe it or not,
you are strong.

i wrote this for you

i miss you, still
no longer in a deep, aching way,
but rather in the dull hum of my car radio

i hope you smiled today

and while you're getting swept up
in the excitement and mystery and
passion of this confusing, intriguing,
heartbreaking, beautiful life

i hope you never forget what is most important

i hope you remember that
it's not about finding someone to complete
and write sappy poems about,
it's not about listening to soft music on repeat
with your eyes closed,
wishing you were somewhere else
or someone else,
and it's not about doing well on exams,
or traveling the world,
or always being artificial sunshine
instead of being real

because it's okay to have sad days,
and a number in the corner of a page
can't give you lasting satisfaction,
and you can't be everyone's prince charming,
and while music stirs up something
so beautiful inside of us,
you can't hide in your melancholy world
of D minor, forever

every night i pray that you're not lost,
that you're somehow finding your way,
and although
i can't speak these words to you directly,
i hope you know
i'll always care.

I'm at the point where I can go from feeling so much to so little in an instant. My emotions are all disarray. I feel like my veins are pumping potential energy, heart beat-beat-beating in anticipation for all the things that are about to happen in my life. Growing up is weird. I'm learning and changing and evolving and it doesn't feel like summer that passes and it's August and you're wondering where all the time went... every day I feel time whizzing past; if the hands on the clock rotate any faster it'll fly off my desk and out the window. I am so many things, and I'm training my eyes to find possibility in every second, to not let time get away from me, to not let myself live in a time that hasn't even come yet. There is so much I want to do, so much I want to see, so much I want to create, so much I want to be. I'm chasing light and I'm discovering who I am and what I want to do and how I want to live and I'm aching to praise my God with every breath.

revitalisation

i fear that you are
drowning in your own depth
and i hope that you have
learned to hold your breath
for extended periods of time
and that you know when
to come up for an interlude
of fresh air every once in awhile

your heart is so
special
please take care
of it

because i would hate
to hear that you've broken
two more

one, hers
and in return, yours
yet again

n o b i g g i e

I love it when I notice others
using the same vocabulary
or phrases as me

And while my mouth may remain
a straight line
in efforts to portray indifference,
my heart is smiling
from beat to beat
because it means that
you held me so close
that a bit of who I am
rubbed off onto you

It makes me feel as though
I'll always be a little part of you,
disguised by letters,
unnoticeable to anyone else

But I see it (I see bits of me in you)

I'm still with you,
and I wonder if you can see it, too

late winter
2014

happiness

Two Februarys ago, all I wanted to do was sleep. I was anchored to my bed with the sadness I was letting myself drown in. Now, I daydream about surviving on 3 hours of sleep, I dread going to bed, I keep my eyes open as long as I can. My heart sinks when the sun sets, I crave daylight; I've fallen in love with being alive.

guarding my heart

i don't want to sit around all day
impatiently waiting for him to call
and when i finally hear his voice
i don't want to feel like he's
the air in my lungs i need to breathe
and when it's time to say goodbye
i don't want to fight over
who should hang up first

i'm not looking for someone
to make me feel whole,
because i already am
i'm not looking for someone
to save me because
i've already been saved

i don't want to be holding
hands at the wrist so if (when)
he lets go, i'm still holding on

i don't want in-between
fake promises from prince charming

i want diner breakfasts
at 3 in the morning and
long car rides with broken radios
and letters written in pen with
nothing scribbled out because
he doesn't care about perfection,
he cares about being real

when it's time,
i want to be in love
not in love
with feeling loved

you will never read this, but i am so sorry

So often I feel as though I am seen as summer rain,
someone who does nothing but
nourishes thirsty flowers in dry soil,
precious and beautiful and unable to do any wrong

when in reality, there are unseen, hidden parts of me
and secrets I've only been brave enough
to whisper to a few, bits of my past
that are journal pages ripped up
and swept underneath my bed

And you are my deepest secret

I took advantage of how you felt for me
and I made you feel like you
were dirt, contaminating me because
I was innocent and perfect and could do no wrong,
but that was a lie I tried to make you believe,
because I had convinced myself
it was true, for so long

I hate that I hurt you

And I hate that I will never
be able to take that back

I cannot stand the thought of you
walking around today, or years from now
thinking of me as a mistake, a waste of time,
a thunderstorm who did nothing but uproot
such special feelings only to
destroy you in your vulnerability

But I pray you don't think of me at all,
and that you've forgotten me

because I cannot stand to think
you're out there, somewhere
remembering me as someone
who broke you

i need to let go

sometimes i call your
number just for a recording
to tell me that it is
no longer in use; you're
gone and i wish i had the
chance to speak to you
just one more time, but
i know that's a wish i'll
waste on shooting stars
for quite a long time

so, i'll see you in songs and
movies that remind me of you;
old poems, the whispering
wind, and my aching heart

maybe i'll see your face
on a crowded sidewalk
one day

or maybe
i'll never hear from you again

"one day"

i'm so hopeful for one day.

from a november letter i never sent

I should've realized it
when you told me
that you didn't know
if you were in love with me,
yet you had no problem
with saying
I love you
over and over
again

b o y

i saw you outside
on my roof tonight
with your messy hair
and cigarette glowing
between your fingertips and
you wouldn't leave but
you wouldn't come in
and i kept staring as you
blew puffs of smoke
with your back against my
bedroom window and
i wanted to get up and crawl
outside and sit behind
you and draw pictures on
your back of all the things
i didn't know how to say but
my blankets felt like lead
so i whispered to my pillow how
much i love you and then
the sun began to rise
and you looked back at me
with ashes beneath your
eyes and i told my pillow
i wish you'd stay
but you didn't you
never do

maybe we get hurt just to heal

I used to pray that I'd never be loved by
anyone I couldn't love back,
but then I remembered how many mountains
I grew strong enough to climb when
you didn't love me back
and I realized that
there's no use in praying for
the absence of pain
because it will always find you
whether it be through sunburns or aching silence
and broken bones grow back stronger
so I won't pray you'll never get hurt
I'll pray you clean out the cuts on your
elbows and learn to not pick at
the scabs on your knees
and that you'll stand up more times
than the wind knocks you down
And that you'll find ways to appreciate
the circles beneath your eyes, but
still hold onto the hope that one day
you will count your scars and smile because
you are proud of how far you've come
and how much you've grown, and
you're not just surviving, you are alive.

11:14

i hope one day
your heart feels what real love is,
i hope you learn that
what you feel now does not
compare to what could be

it's not crazy infatuation,
constantly trying to catch your breath
no sanity, recklessness

what you're feeling is
the need to feel loved by someone
who isn't truly loving you

but i hope one day
you'll find that love doesn't mean
crying and screaming and aching,
left lifeless from all the pain,
it means patience and trust and
kindness and selflessness and
it won't always be easy, but you
won't have to lie awake at night, afraid
that he won't love you in the morning
because he won't treat your heart
like clay in his hands

you're letting yourself go crazy
because you're afraid
you wouldn't know
how to deal
with the pain
if you were sane

you may think that this insanity is sacrifice,
but don't give your heart to someone
who requires you to lose your mind

collecting dust

it's difficult
to romanticize the past
or even
remember it as genuine
when i keep discovering
more and more each day
that everything
you said,
and everything you
promised,
and everything
i thought was true,
was not

does his love make your head spin?

when i asked if he had any tattoos, he said
not yet. but if i do, it'll be to do with God or you.

it has been
76 days
since he
scratched
out
my name
from
his heart
and moved
onto
you

it'll be to do with God or you.

i wonder if that line gave you butterflies, too.

n o t e s

3:07am
i miss you every day
not who you are today,
but who you used to be

6:11am
i think you come and visit me
in the middle of the night
because i keep waking up
with scratches on my back

6:12pm
if i'd known that'd be the last time we'd speak,
i would've never gone to sleep

3:24am
i miss you so much
i don't know why, but i do
and it hurts so much at night
and i wish i'd saved my photographs of you
i miss you, i miss you, i miss you

rope swings

i found you
but you've found
someone else
so i will not let you know

i'm choking on
questions like
was i foolish for
thinking your heart
could still beat for me?
and
am i selfish for
wishing it did?

i found you
but i know
you are better off
with me hiding
in the trees

i will not let you know

l i m e r e n c e

i guess you only like girls who are broken
and want to be hurt, like your hands
around her neck, want
bruises and cuts
in the shape of a heart,
inhaling and choking on your affection
like she needs it to breathe

translucent skin stretched across
veins that pump nicotine and you
you, you, you, you, you

judgment clouded by hyper-dependent
infatuation and the need to heal her
hollowness, although you'll only ever
be another teardrop on her pillowcase
while she hums herself to sleep
with midnight lies

"the loss of you would be the loss of my life"

and the saddest part
is that i almost let myself fall
back into becoming that
lifeless, empty girl
once more because i thought it might
make you love me again

are, our

one time when i was eight
i slept over at my friend's house
and that night we held back
her mom's hair as she got sick
over a broken heart
into a trashcan at
the foot of her bed
and i didn't understand
how someone could be so sad
but right now, lying
on the bathroom floor
getting sick over you, i do.

d r e a m t

i dreamt you could love me again,
that you had a big studio apartment in the city
and you bought her lots of gifts,
made her go thrifting with you
to buy strange clothes,
but she knew you loved someone else,
she knew you missed me
and that you would always be mine,
and although i woke up
and not a bit of it was true
(because i know you love her
and that you don't think about me)
it was still nice to live in a world
where your heart had not
forgotten my name

flesh

i'm still in love with you and it's hard to admit that to myself, but i am and i know i am and i know it's not healthy and it's not what i want, but i am in love with you and i crave your fingertips on my skin and your whisper in my ear and your silent presence and your obsessive thoughts. i selfishly miss the way you used to love me, like sitting at the edge of a bridge over stormy waters. i miss your insanity and your venom and your beating heart. i daydream about holding your hand as you smoke on the crowded sidewalk and drinking coffee creamer with you at 4am and waking up with street-lights peaking through the blinds and being with you in a city that doesn't care about me, the same way you don't care about me, but even if you wanted me, i'd still run away. you love someone now who is beautiful and hates herself and i secretly wish sometimes you make her cry by sighing my name into her mouth. but i know she's all you see and that you've left me behind where i should be because i ripped you apart and i'd do it again, because i know i can't handle loving you and that i'd hurt you and me over and over again. but it's hard to hurt someone who doesn't care. and i don't want to. i rather scream into my pillow every night and tolerate the pain of wanting you so badly, and not even being able to tell you, than let you know i love you. i can't hurt you again. i can't let you hurt me again. i love you. i love you. i love you. i don't want to. you don't love me. i love you.

a collection of obsession

2:54 PM
i want to cry but the tears won't come

3:19 PM
and at this moment in time
i do not know
if i'd be strong enough
to turn you away

9:46 PM
i'd let you break my heart again
and the cracks would be in the shape
of bittersweet grins

11:35 PM
call me baby and tell me i look like the sky at dusk

5:16 PM
you used to love me

3:33 AM
now, you are real to me
i'm sorry it took me so long

3:47 AM
it's raining and i love you

4:11 PM
now i know how it felt and i'm so sorry

11:45 PM
out of everyone on the planet
i only wish i could talk to you

12:34 AM
and you haven't even touched me

9:37 PM
i read all words in your voice

7:36 PM
i don't want to be sad about you forever

9:34 PM
everyone moves on but me

1:05 AM
they're all gone there is no one

4:02 AM
goodnight, i miss you

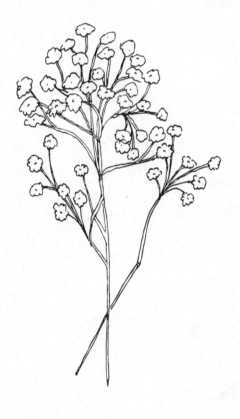

spring & summer
2014

the queen of burning bridges

is it new york i love
or do i crave being
near you; crave the
one in a million
chance that if we
were in the same city
we would run into
each other on the
sidewalk while i'm
on my way to buy
flowers and you're
smoking a cigarette
dressed in all black
and i'd smile at you
and you'd grab me by
the wrists and scold
me for being away
for so long and then
i'd let you kiss my face
as you interlock your
fingers with mine and
you'd never let me go
again, you would
take me with you
wherever you went
and i'd never look back

05/16/14

i feel hollow. the things i feel, i wish so badly to disappear, i refuse to let them out, i hide them in the deepest parts of me, in hopes that i may trick myself into believing they are not there at all. i keep pen and paper out of reach, i haven't cried in weeks, because feelings that aren't there (they aren't there, i don't feel a thing) can't make you cry. i keep telling myself i am hollow, because for some reason that seems better than admitting i am full of poetry i refuse to write.

a text to a friend
who doesn't realize his worth

outside, the rain is pouring and each drop is whispering to me how lovely you are. it rolls down the roof and seeps into the soil, creating a song in the darkness as it falls onto the pavement. my room is dim except for the streetlight peaking through the window over my desk. all the little moments happening to create this moment right now are individually necessary and beautiful. you are rain falling. you are shadows on my bedroom walls. you are subtle light. you are so many things. but all you are allowing yourself to focus on is the dirt beneath the grass, the leaking in the shingles. but i'm lying in my bed staring at the ceiling and all i can think about is how lovely it is to fall asleep to the sound of rain. you are many things, all necessary, all beautiful. and i see it. one day you will, too.

the cry of my heart

My heart beats for Your glory
I want to love You more
My eyes search for emptiness
to fill with Your fullness
I want to love You more
My lips tingle to occupy silence
with the knowledge of Your holiness
I want to love You more
My feet stumble, they wander left
when I'm shouting at them to go right
I want to love You more
My hands tremble and hide inside
my pockets instead of reaching out
to bring You praise
My sinful flesh needs You
I want to love You more

i am not a shadow

i don't want to be someone who writes in pencil
and eats too slowly and walks with eyes that
are glued to the sidewalk and tops of strangers' feet

i've been underwater for so long that
i've forgotten lungs are meant
to be filled with air; exhaling seems
more like something found
on the second star to the right, rather
than a process that is meant to be
done twenty-three thousand times a day

i feel like an old woman who
looks in the mirror and all she can see
are wrinkles and white hair and tired eyes and
the absence of who she used to be

but i am not someone who turns away
from sunsets and pretends
that darkness is all i've ever known;
someone who thinks
the sun will never rise again

because the sun will rise again—
the words hiding inside of me will
find their way out, because
i cannot hold my breath forever

i am not someone who writes in pencil
and erases the bits that are too
honest and too imperfect and too real
to claim as thoughts of my own

i cannot keep my lips pursed and
hands tied behind my back,
i cannot keep pretending i am
a shadow of who i used to be

my tomorrows hold suns much
brighter than ones that have risen
over horizons of my past;
i have not reached the summit yet

there is so much more me
for me to become

each day, i am new.

when silence speaks

i've been suppressing so much
hurt without realizing it,
deep cuts i didn't even know
were there to heal,
and now it's all coming up
and it's terrifying
to feel this way again
and to not be able to breathe,
but at the same time,
it's so comforting to know
my heart isn't made of stone

we're looking at the same stars

I think the scent of bug spray on my palms will now forever remind me of you and the late night (early morning) we spent sitting in your car, drawing awfully unskillful portraits on the back of each other's hands in dim light and 3 a.m. stillness. (I wonder if you could tell that doodling on your skin was just an excuse to touch you.) I wanted so badly to let my fingers find yours as we laid back in our seats and peeked out the rolled down windows at the infinite stars scattered above us in the early August night sky. I told you I wouldn't kiss you, because I know my heart and how relentlessly it would replay how your lips felt on mine, and how it would ache knowing you couldn't be mine, so I let you kiss my cheek instead, and the half a moment that I felt your unshaven face brush mine in the middle of the street at five in the morning feels like a fake memory. When you looked at me, I wanted to hide, because I was too afraid to read what words might've been written in your eyes, but I felt so content listening to the deep tone of your voice mix with the obnoxiously loud crickets singing in the trees surrounding us. I could've sat there with you till the stars disappeared and the sun took their place, but you walked me back home, and you left in the dark, and now I'm sitting in my bed thinking about how the hours between 2 and 5 a.m. have never felt so full.

sorry we never went putt-putting, have fun kissing other girls

i thought it'd be poetic
to leave you the same way i found you,
with a contentless text—
a simple entered space
(i knew you wouldn't catch it)
although you seem to be someone
who thinks very deeply about all someones,
your thoughts about me are puddles
disguised as over-complimenting oceans

and i really do not know
what i am or what i've been to you,
or if i'll be able to keep myself away
from you, or why you'd drive hours
to see me in the middle of the night
when you "plan on kissing at least one
girl in the next three months,"
(couldn't care less if it's me)

"what would i be waiting for?" you asked.

i'm barefoot, chasing a train i know
is on tracks that lead away from where
i want and need to be (but i liked the way
it felt when your hand touched mine)

glad i never gave you any piece of my heart,
because you're the type of boy who'd
rip it to shreds, hide your claws
behind your back, and tell me that
i should've seen it coming
(though you would've been right)

maybe you're just bored,
and that's why you decorate
your skin with ink and don't care

about whose lips you've touched,
and i wish i could figure you out,
wish i could draw a perfect portrait
with my words (or even just
my thoughts) of who you are,
but i won't pretend i know you

i hate you and your pansy tattoo
(but i don't really hate you,
i hate the way i let you make me feel.)

autumn
2014

i'm just as broken as you are

i don't know how someone as small as me
with bones that break at the sight of heat lightning
and heart strings that thread apart at the sound of his voice
could make anyone feel like the sun shines brighter
through kaleidoscope eyes—
you're okay if it brings out the freckles on your face,
and you feel good, you feel alive
you say i showed you how to love in a new way,
that i taught you to be so much more okay with your tummy,
"it's been very freeing and life is a lot better, thank you,"
but i feel like i can't say *you're welcome* because
i am a messy cliché of imperfect scraps and hypocrisy
loosely sewn together with
you are strong, you are strong, you are strong
but i feel so weak i feel so weak i feel so weak
and i am not steady hands, they shake like
wet dogs after kiddy pool baths,
i am flower seeds that forgot how to bloom, trapped
below the surface of a garden that feels like quicksand
and i'm sorry but you don't see all the mistakes i make,
all the words i've preached that look back at me
and laugh when they see
what i feel, what i think, who i am behind closed doors,
i'm sorry.
you keep hanging medals around my neck, and
they're so heavy, and i don't know
what to say besides *i love you*
when you speak words of adoration,
but please do not praise me, i am not good.

2:20 AM

The words I can't say to you are
climbing up my throat
I keep forgetting to breathe
I miss your hands.

i don't know who i am right now, but let's pretend i do

i want to dye
my hair and tattoo my skin
so that the changes
you've been noticing in me
look like they're
on purpose

8 word story

i wanted you to love me on purpose.

what kept me up last night

03:00
When I think about never speaking to him again, I picture a girl walking in a crowd that's all moving in the same direction, and then suddenly she drops everything she's holding and turns around and starts running as fast as she can, smiling and pushing past everyone till finally she reaches an open space and her face looks like sunshine as her hair blows behind her in the wind and she's free, she's free, oh God, she's free.

03:15
But then I think about walking into a doctor's office ten years from now and sitting on a cold metal table, staring at my legs dangling off the edge, waiting. And then I look up as the door opens slowly, not expecting to see his tattooed arms hidden in a white coat, but there he is and, oh God, his eyes haven't changed, and I can't breathe, and he just stands there, looking at me like an unfinished sentence. Then I'd have to let him put a stethoscope to my chest and listen to my heart, and I wonder what it'd sound like, if it would sound like messy half beats of missing him. If he'd be able to tell. If he'd care.

03:30
Or maybe the next time I see him, if I ever see him again, we'll both be whole versions of ourselves, content and in good places, our lives all sorted out and how we always hoped they'd be. And maybe we'd be able to talk about the weather and our kids and the lives we created apart. And maybe I'd be able to look at him with only feelings of pleasant acquaintance and relative indifference, not seeing the boy I fell for when I should've been focused on catching myself.

03:45
And I know I should find comfort in thinking about how one day I may look at him and feel nothing,

04:00
but it's four in the morning and I don't want to let go.

how to not care

he's telling me about the girl at school
he can't get out of his head,
and how he feels like
it's always this chain of
"i don't want all these people that want me,"
(i winced)
"and the one person i want doesn't want me
in the same way."
(i inhaled sharply)

i told him he's overthinking it,
and when he asked, "how do you not?"
(i forgot to breathe)

my eyes got watery, but i blinked quickly
before they could settle
(i exhaled)

and replied,
"i'll let you know."

such a sinking feeling

i've never had feelings for anyone who was good for me. i've never been interested in someone where a good, healthy relationship could've resulted, and maybe that's why i'm so jaded, because everyone i've ever liked has just been a distraction or a house on fire—someone i know i shouldn't be involved with, but i'll give myself just a few more days to run around frantically with my hands over my eyes, peeking through the cracks between my fingers, searching for things i know i don't really need, and then i'll dash out and run down the driveway, and the smog will linger for a little while, and the neighbors will complain, and i'll sit on the curb with my forehead on my knees, holding nothing but intangible regret.

next, i'll either get over it, or obsessively think about him and the ashes smudged on the inside of my eyelids for longer than my sanity. i've never really liked someone and been able to daydream about the real possibility of us turning into something greater; of tire swings and painted mailboxes and overgrown, green lawns. it's always been pretending and fake hope and melodramatic doom. i think it's messed up my perception of having feelings for someone, because i can never take it seriously— either i know he's not right for me, or i know the circumstances prohibit the possibility of us. it makes me never want to give anyone a chance (i can't even see anyone worth chance-giving) because i know how it ends. i don't like having this closed off heart so early on; i'm too young to be this bitter.

twenty word explanation

ask me how many boys have told me they loved me, then ask me how many of them meant it.

go away, i'll be okay

it's unsettling how many people i've had to beg to forget me, lately. how many i've tried to convince that i really am as insignificant as a stranger you made eye contact with for a moment at the stoplight. for so long i was begging so many people to stay, to keep holding onto me, even if it wasn't in their best interest. all i wanted was to be selfishly adored. now all i want is to be left alone.

butterflies, trains, and blood stains

you didn't like the way i answered the phone,
and you thought it was gross that i liked mushrooms on my
pizza,
and you told me i was weird-looking when i was a kid,
and once i sent you a photo of a tattoo and you said you
didn't like it, you didn't know they were my words that were
written on her skin

you told me what "too much damage" meant on halloween
after all the trick-or-treaters had fallen asleep
and when i kept silent for three days after,
and winced at every kissing scene on television, because
they flooded the insides of my eyelids with images that made
me feel very small,
you said i was being unfair
because i was the one who decided we were just friends,
and i told you we weren't, you knew we weren't
we couldn't be after what we used to be

i told you i still had feelings that hadn't gone away yet,
you said they hadn't gone away for you either

i pictured you holding my hand

but then you said,
"that's why it's easier to run from them
and hide in other girls' beds."

you always told me every thought
that popped into your head, and i used to find it endearing,
i kept telling myself that you deserved my ear,
but i really hope you have nothing more to say
because, i promise, i'm done listening

so clear off your bedside table, and cut the
blue string that's wrapped around your wrist if you've yet to
do so,
and stop asking me if i miss you,
because this is me saying
i don't.

see you there

i think we still exist
somewhere in the universe
behind the sun
where all of earth's abandoned
soulmates go to rest

i think i can see us
when i look up at the sky
and squint directly into
the rays of light,
your brown eyes burning
into mine

i think we are together
in the time that trails behind
the present, dancing
in circles until the last stars
fizzle out

i think that our promises
seeped into the soil, like
february rain, our souls sown
together, tucked in
beneath the world

i think what we had is
somewhere just out of reach,
pulsing in the dim spaces
between heat lightning

and although, in this lifetime,
we became nothing but shadows,
monsters that linger on bedroom walls

we are there, we are alive,
and we are still in love

you again

are hands and knees that hit the floor
and crawl back towards what i'd sworn off before
weak, or brave
is it braver to run in the opposite direction
or to stay even when it stings
because when we're in your car
i know what the crickets outside
are thinking, is it true
am i throwing white sheets over old reminders
written in dust, small whispers leading up
to an attic where all the hurt and confusion is stored
in cardboard boxes labelled DO NOT OPEN

right now i'm sitting on the stairs
with my back against the door
and i'm looking at your face, your face, your face
searching for something maybe i didn't see before
and the words you wrote at two in the dark
made me miss you when i promised i didn't,
and i want to stay, but when i try
to convince myself that you're right,
that pushing you away is the easy way out,
that what we feel is a reason to keep each
other around,
i still find it hard to believe myself
when i tell myself
that i am being strong

two weeks

i'm always all too conscious
of moments hanging in the air

like watching helium balloons slowly
fall down the wall to cover the ground,
i keep stepping on them till they pop

like looking out the window once the sun starts to set
and you can't see the light fading, but then you
blink and you're sitting in a dark room

sitting next to you
with eyes closed and breath held
in a moment
that doesn't feel real

like i'm looking down at the earth
while standing on the moon

and i know i'll miss it once it's gone,
but i can't seem to figure out
how to freeze the hours that feel like seconds
passing by and

then it's time to leave
and i held your hand while you drove me home,
thinking about how real everything felt
with the lights blurring past on the interstate,
how i wanted the road to go on forever,
watching you rap stupid songs and
talk about how to feel grown up
without really growing up
and then suddenly

it was gone, like it was never there

and i sat on my bed
wishing i could walk back into
the hands on the clock and
your hands on my face, but it
disappeared, floated up to the ceiling
carrying my heart with it

and all i have now are
memories that feel like dreams

to play back in my head
until time fades back into you

winter
2014-2015

letters to You

It's been three and a half months since we last spoke,
really spoke, not just guilty hellos
and scattered half-hearted pleas

And it's not you, it's never you
it's me it's me it's me,
but you love
me
you love
me
you love
me

And my head has forgotten what it feels like,
but I know my heart is safe with you

Because you've never stopped chasing after me
and I'm tired of looking at my feet, telling myself
I'll be okay without you, trying to navigate
through a thick forest at night,
pretending I don't have matches at
my fingertips

You are the only thing
that has ever made me feel truly whole

I'm sorry I've kept my eyes shut so tight,
but I'm here now and I love you and I miss you

And I don't want to keep living
like fragments of a person anymore

I'm Yours.

it was a wednesday

afternoon light shining in through the sheer curtains hanging over my bedroom window, on the most ordinary day of the week, your arms were around me and my head was on your chest as it slowly rose and fell, and you twitch as you're falling asleep, and i never thought i could fall in love with the sound of someone snoring, but your sleepy inhales made my heart swell, and since then, the day has been a series of heavy exhales. i can feel the weight of you behind my ribs and in the corners of my mouth as i smile at the thought of kissing you, your laugh, the way your eyes look when they're looking at me, the sound of your voice when you're trying to get music to play in your car, how i feel when i can feel you next to me; i hope you don't mind, but no matter what time or space is between us, you've written your name in the sand of my soul and no amount of wind or waves will ever be able to wash it away. the time we've spent together feels like seconds, but you will always exist in my memory as someone who held my hand as i walked into the sun.

my eyes are closed

i want to dissolve into the sky
without a sound
without anyone noticing my empty space
in the most gentle and subtle way possible
i want to go away from here
i want to walk backwards and save myself
from what inevitability is ahead
i want to leave
i want you
to wish i'd stay

lingering daydreams

i hate that i'm lying in bed
with a cup of tea
and can see myself in the future
in our bed
with a cup of tea
and you lying next to me

and i hate that i can see myself turning out the light
and laying my head to rest
on your chest

i hate that i can see us sitting at a little round kitchen table
next to the window
you in your black rimmed glasses
scrolling through your phone
me with my hair tied up and one knee drawn up to my chest,
eating a bowl of oatmeal as the sun creeps its way
into the middle of the sky

i hate that i can see us side by side
brushing our teeth in a cramped bathroom
in front of a foggy mirror,
listening to music as we get ready for the day

i hate that i can see us walking out the front door,
i hate that i can see us kissing goodbye

because i'm lying in bed
with a cup of tea
thinking about all of this,
thinking about you

yet i've already
kissed you
goodbye

it's so frustrating because i know you wanted to be with me, on those days you drove almost an hour each way to see me and you kissed me so often and held me so tight and always pulled me closer and i could feel your eyes on me when i wasn't looking, and we spent day after day like this, just being together and pretending that time could stand still, but at the same time, i feel like it was all just something for you to do while you were home, even though you deny it. i remember starting to tear up one afternoon with my head on your chest while you slept, because i knew it was just a matter of time till this was just a memory. i can't picture you actually missing me, i can't imagine you actually wishing i hadn't said i was done with grey and in between. i feel like i'm so insignificant to you. like you have no feelings, like you couldn't care less, this is just life, people come and go. and i know that, i know this is just life, and that people come and go, but it hurts that it'd never cross your mind to ask me to stay, that i was fun while i lasted, that you never wanted to make me yours. i'll fade soon. i want to matter more to you. you're a thinker, i'm a feeler, you hate that i'm so black and white. but i'm selfish and i want 3am texts that you can't stop thinking about me and that you need to see me again soon. but that's not who you are. and it's unfair of me to want you to feel that way when you don't. and it's really okay, because if i extended my hand to you and you took it, i don't think we would've gotten very far, anyway. i loved being so close to you, but i'm excited to hold someone's hand who doesn't want to let go, to kiss someone who wants to kiss me forever, to not be anticipating an inevitable end, to be able to trust someone fully with my heart, to have someone that wants to hold it. and i don't need that, i don't need someone, i don't need anyone. but if one day it's what's meant to be, i'll let it be. i don't want to be careless with my heart again. i don't know why things happen the way they do, and i don't regret you for a second, and i still think the world of you, but i'm too emotional and i fall too deep to give that much of myself again to someone who never asked for any of it in the first place.

just friends (some friend)

my stomach is in knots
and i feel so sick thinking about you
holding anyone that isn't me
and i don't understand why you thought it'd be a good idea
to tell me that you're falling asleep at night
with another girl in your bed,
even if you're not kissing her goodnight,
i tried to drown out my sobs all day with
modern vampires of the city on vinyl,
but it still feels like someone
sunk fangs in my lungs

it's only been a week, the cuts from your nails
from holding my heart so tight
are still fresh
and i never asked you to stop,
i never told you i wanted to try
to be more than friends again,
i never tried to paint your hands red,
but all you could seem to do is defend
yourself and repeat that you've done nothing wrong
you said we're just friends
you said we're just friends
you said we're just friends

and we are just friends,
i just wanted you to understand and acknowledge
that it still hurts

and you can say you're sorry, you said sorry,
but i'm sure she's tucked in beneath your sheets right now
and you're still repeating in your head,
"i've done nothing wrong"

we're just friends
we're just friends
we're just friends

and i'm glad you're comfortable,
i'm glad you know you've done nothing wrong,
i'm glad you have someone to hold at night,
i'm glad thoughts of me don't rip your heart out,
i'm glad you're okay with being just friends

i'm glad you're fine

but, i'm sorry,
i'm not.

indigo

you are the song
i want to listen to
in that cliché and timeless
3am moment on the highway
windows rolled
down with the
potential-filled and empty
yet comforting indigo
sky blowing past,
only car on the road
just us, me with my
feet up on the dash,
fingers interlocked with
yours on my lap,
headlights illuminating
the road and trees
ahead, can't think about
anything else except
for the pulse of the night
and cold air on my skin
and oh God
this is my life and
i feel so alive

midnight journal

It terrifies me that we only get a limited amount of time with people. And that some people get more time than others who should have. I'm forever envious of those who've gotten more time with you than I have. That I may never get to be with you as long as they have. That our time is running out. And I miss you already. And I never want to say goodbye. At first it was slow, late nights in your car and afternoons in my bedroom. But now it feels like it's happening all at once, like you're doing a snow angel on my heart and it keeps getting bigger and bigger. Kissing on the sidewalk, holding hands in your coat pocket because I forgot to bring gloves. Wandering around museums and having hard conversations on your couch that make me love you even more; even when the air becomes glass, I can't stop thinking about how lucky I feel to know you. That there's no one else like you. My heart aches in your arms and aches when we're apart. And I just want to be as close to you as possible, for as long as possible, because you are the most beautiful person I've ever met, and I love who I am when I'm with you.

love me all the way

I wonder how different life would be if I wasn't living in the confines of how someone else thinks I should live. I'm dreaming of a world where I have the freedom to figure things out on my own without smothering eyes piercing every inch of my flesh. A world where I'm loved without bullet point conditions, where I'm not afraid of what you'd think, because you should know I'm human and everything is grey and confusing and please don't act like you have it all together and that you never have doubts and that everything makes sense. Nothing makes sense. I've misplaced my convictions. and I don't want to let go of what I've felt in my heart for so long, but I don't want to keep holding onto it just because it's what is expected of me. I don't want to live a life of obligation. I don't want to live a life of apathy. I don't want to be someone just because that's who you think I should be. I want to be who I think I should be. And all I know is that I should be me. Just me. Let me wander down different paths and stare up at the sky and trip over my own feet till I end up where I'm meant to be. Don't tell me where to go, or how to get there, because I will run in the opposite direction of your hands that are grabbing at my ankles, trying to drag me into the sun. I don't want to take the easy way out. I'll get to where I'm supposed to be going, and when I get there, I want it to be real. I want to be running towards it with outstretched arms and faith that blankets mountains. I'll get there. Don't carry me. Just love me all the way.

spring
2015

kathleen

I am slowly learning to disregard the insatiable desire to be special. I think it began, the soft piano ballad of epiphanic freedom that danced in my head, when you mentioned that "Van Gogh was her thing" while I stood there in my overall dress, admiring his sunflowers at the art museum. And then again on South Street, while we thumbed through old records and I picked up Morrissey and you mentioned her name like it was stuck in your teeth. Each time, I felt a paintbrush on my cheeks, covering my skin in grey and fading me into a quiet, concealed background that hummed *everything you've ever loved has been loved before, and everything you are has already been* on an endless loop. It echoed in your wrists that I stared at, walking (home) in the middle of the street, and I felt like a ghost moving forward in an eternal line, waiting to haunt anyone who thought I was worth it. But no one keeps my name folded in their wallet. Only girls who are able to carve their names into paintings and vinyl live in pockets and dust bunnies and bathroom mirrors. And so be it, that I am grey and humming in the background. I am forgotten Sundays and chipped fingernail polish and borrowed sheets. I'm the song you'll get stuck in your head, but it will remind you of someone else. I am 2 in the afternoon, I am the last day of winter, I am a face on the sidewalk that won't show up in your dreams. And I am everywhere, and I am nothing at all.

in a good way

it's like time is moving one step ahead of you when you're together and you can't keep up and the hands on the clock are spinning so fast that it tangles your hair and sunsets mix with sunrises and nights spent listening to each other breathe all start to blend together and it feels like this is how life's always been, you and him, and you can't remember the last time you felt so happy being woken up at 8am because he's kissing you goodbye, or so okay with staring at the ceiling at three in the morning because you're not alone

and
 suddenly

he's gone, but he's still there, just not in the same way. and all you can do is hide beneath your covers and from yourself or in public places and from everyone else, with your tissues that aren't so obvious because it's spring and pollen's dusting every surface it can reach, but that's not the only reason your eyes are bloodshot. you're trying so hard not to play back every moment you spent together in your head, and you don't want to erase the photos because you don't want to let them win, and you don't want to forget, and things that existed before he existed to you remind you of him and it isn't fair at all that going to the grocery store can make you want to cry. and you keep telling yourself you shouldn't feel so sad, that you need to let go because this is just how it goes. and you miss him, but you can't, because the sunsets that fell so quickly when you were wrapped up in his arms are slow now, moving down the sky like a thick milkshake you can't suck through a straw, and all the colors of the sky are mixing together and painting words that you can read with your eyes closed, and it is this—that it is over, and you will never get it back.

atoms

i've given up on days that begin in late afternoon,
skipped breakfast and lunch,
days that fade slowly and end with
bloody cut-out holes in eyelids because
the second i close them and it all goes black,
every moment with you comes back
played on fast-forward, the memories moving so quickly
that both our faces are blurred
and it feels like everything i've ever felt for you
is overflowing the tub, filling the washroom with
suds that take forever to melt

i've given up on those days.

i've traded them for ones that begin with
sunrises instead of sunsets,
days that are spent falling forward
instead of trying to chase the past, and i don't
look back and see something broken, or
something that was better off left unopened

i look back and see our bodies so close together
that you can't tell where yours begins and mine ends,
i see my heart that grew twenty-three times its size,
i see you and me wrapped up in something that
i didn't know existed outside of blurry 35 mm
and overdue and falling-apart library books
that sit on the nightstands of middle-aged women
who are bored with their lives

and i'm just so happy i got to love you at all.

but i've folded up all the days spent with you
and taped them in the messy pages of my journal
and now i'm running into the sun,
running away from every lie that's trying to

wedge its way in between my ribs,
running in the opposite direction of words like "regret"
and any feeling that insists that none of it was worth it

because all of it was worth it.

every moment we were together pumps
through my veins, and it will always be there;
it will be there when we've both graduated,
when you move out west,
when you kiss your family goodnight
when you sit in your backyard with tears
in your eyes because you've lived a life
you are proud of

it will be there when i finally make it to new york city,
when i kiss someone who isn't you,
when i find the answers you inspired me to search for,
when i sit on my rooftop with tears on my cheeks
because i've lived a life fuller than i could've ever imagined

and you and i will live these lives apart,
we'll move on and forget what it felt like
to wake up beside one another;
we'll find what we're looking for elsewhere
and we'll understand why this all had to happen the way that
it did

but what we had will always exist somewhere,
in rotting apples and old mail and unplayed mix CDs,
in mosaics that line the city streets, in sirens and
red and white flashing lights that shine through
your window while you are asleep

you and i were magic,
we always will be.

you are going to miss people

you are going to miss people

you'll want to get out of bed at two in the morning
and drive to go see them
you'll call them even though they changed their number
10 months ago just to hear a dial tone
you'll write letters to them they'll never read,
seal them in envelopes and address them
and stick them in your desk drawer
you'll catch your wandering afternoon thoughts
bumping into old memories that feel warm at first
but then start to sting
you'll lie awake at night trying to remember
and trying to forget what it felt like to fall asleep
knowing they were thinking of you

you are going to miss people

sometimes their hearts will beat the same as yours
and sometimes you'll put your head to their chest
and won't hear a thing
you'll wipe away the hurt from the tops of your cheeks
because they feel so far away

you are going to miss people

you'll get out of bed at two in the morning and dance till
you're not sad anymore
you'll delete old voicemails to make room for new ones
without thinking twice
you'll mail the letters worth mailing and throw away the rest
you'll neglect to notice their name hasn't crossed your mind
in weeks, but when it does you'll smile or feel nothing and it
won't feel empty at all
you'll put your head on your pillow and close your eyes
and sleep will find you before they can

you are going to miss people
you are going to miss people
you are going to miss people

and you are going to be okay.

Acknowledgements

Firstly, thank you Laura Supnik for the beautiful illustrations that decorate this book. It would not feel complete without them. I am so grateful for having such a talented friend who was willing to work with my scatterbrain. You are as lovely as the flowers you draw.

Thank you to anyone who inspired the pieces in this book, whether they were happy or sad. They've led me to find and love who I truly am and I wouldn't change a thing. I've learned so much over these past few years, and both the mountains and valleys have contributed to the sense of strength I feel in my bones today.

Cliché, but necessary, thank you to my family—Mom, Dad, Natalie, Jake, and Angel (woof.) You've held me close through it all. Thanks for dealing with the moodiness and the angst of my teen years. You are golden.

And last, but not least, to those whom this book of poetry is dedicated to. To the ones that read my dramatic late night blog posts, favorite my weirdo tweets, comment on my Instagram selfies, and watch my sporadic YouTube videos. To the ones who understand and feel these words on a deep and personal level, a level that has created a special, unbreakable, and eternal bond between us—

Thank you.
Thank you written on a ginormous ice cream cake,
 room filled floor to ceiling with balloons,
fireworks in the sky,
and an endless supply of bear hugs.

Thank you in the biggest way possible. This book would not exist without you. Your love has inspired me to take my messy journal entries and turn them into something so much bigger than I could've ever imagined. I'm so glad we have each other.

All my love,

m.k.

index

spring (2013)

summer (2013)

autumn & winter (2013)

about the author
@madisenkuhn • *m.k.* • *madisen.co*

Madisen Kuhn, popularly known as *m.k.* by those who enjoy her writing, was born on the last day of winter in 1996. She has been posting her thoughts and feelings online since 2012, originally on Tumblr, and has since branched out to other platforms, such as Instagram and YouTube. When she isn't writing, she loves blogging, eating cinnamon apple oatmeal, traveling via train, wandering around museums, having late night dance parties in her room, cuddling with her Yorkshire Terrier named Angel, and watching movies with her siblings, Natalie and Jake. She is currently pursuing a Bachelor of Fine Arts degree in Graphic Design. This is her first book.

connect with madisen!

twitter @madisenkuhn
instagram @madisenkuhn
youtube /madisenkuhn
tumblr madisenkuhn.info
pinterest /madisenkuhn

for press/media inquiries and other collaborations, contact mk@madisen.co

connect with laura!

twitter   @laurasupnik
instagram   @laurasupnik
pinterest   /laurasupnik
facebook   /laurasupnikart
website   laurasupnik.com

for inquiries, commissions, and other collaborations, contact lsupnik@gmail.com

you are not where you are from,
you are where you're going

m.k.